100 *of* EXPERIENCES KAZAKHSTAN

HERTFORDSHIRE PRESS

HERTFORDSHIRE PRESS LTD © 2014
Suite 419,
Devonshire Business Centres
Hamilton House
111 Marlowes
Hemel Hempstead
HP1 1BB, UK
www.hertfordshirepress.com

100 EXPERIENCES OF KAZAKHSTAN

Authors: Vitaly Shuptar, Nick Rowan, Dr. Kairat Zakiryanov, Rodger Chao, Dagmar Schreiber

Editor: Nick Rowan

We express our sincere gratitude to the photographers who contributed their photographs for use in this project: Vitaly Shuptar, Alexandr Yermolyonok, Mary O'Connor, Aleksandr Petrov, Vera Voronova, Dagmar Schreiber, Natalya Frankovskaya, Michael Kamper, Yelena Kim, Botagoz Krambayeva, Zh.Kairakhanov, Andrey Yurchenkov, Victor Zaibert, Saltore Saparbaev, Alexander Ivasenko, Xander Casey.

Published in partnership with the Kazakh Academy of Sport and Tourism

ISBN: 978-0-9927873-5-6

First Edition

KAZAKHSTAN

Area:	2,724,900 km2 (9th largest country)
Population:	17,736,896 (July 2013)
Capital:	Astana, (Almaty largest city)
Ethnic groups:	63.1% Kazakh, 23.6% Russian, 2.8% Uzbek, 2.9% Ukrainian, 1.5% German 1.4% Uyghur, 1.3% Tatar, 4.3% others
Languages:	Kazakh (national), Russian
Climate:	The Climate in Kazakhstan is continental. In summer the temperatures average more than 30 °C (86 °F) and in winter average −20 °C (−4.0 °F).
Currency:	Tenge (KZT)

Nick Rowan
Editor, 100 Experiences of Kazakhstan
Editor-in-Chief, Open Central Asia Magazine

Foreword

Twenty years ago, few people in Europe would have been able to name the newly independent Central Asian states, let alone place them on a map. For Kazakhstan, one such state to have gained independence from the USSR on 16th December 1991, the outside world only gave it the faintest of recognition until, in the aftermath of the September 11th 2001 terrorist attacks on the US, western politicians suddenly declared the strategic importance of Central Asia in their war on terror in Afghanistan.

Western businessmen had quietly been building links and investing in Kazakhstan, mainly seeking to grab a share of its nascent but high resource potential oil and gas industry. However, to the ordinary person on the streets of London, Paris, Rome or Washington Kazakhstan remained one of those "Stans," whose name was as difficult to pronounce as its location was to find on the map. By 2006, the country gained unwelcome notoriety with Sasha Baron Cohen's mockumenatry, "Borat", portraying a fictitious Kazakh journalist travelling through the United States and recording real-life and unscripted interactions with ignorant Americans, who were more the focus of mockery than Kazakhstan's portrayal. Despite the initial, and understandable, outrage in Kazakhstan itself, US Kazakh Ambassador, Erlan Idrissov, came out saying that he had found parts of the film funny and wrote that the film had "placed Kazakhstan on the map." By 2012 tourist visas were up tenfold, with the film being credited for helping attract curious travellers to the country.

Today's Kazakhstan can arguably boast a leading position amongst Central Asian nations in the resurgence of importance of former Soviet Republic states. As the world's ninth largest country it is fast shedding its reputation as one of the great travel unknowns as more people explore the great variety of this vast country's attractions. The exotic wilds of the country quickly eradicate the Borat association as visitors find cosmopolitan cities such as Almaty and Astana situated next to the dramatic mountain slopes of the Tien Shan and historical sites of Shymkent and Otrar. The country is fast reinventing itself as a modern nation at the heart of Eurasia with quality hotels, boutique restaurants and a centre of commerce that represents a unique mix of Islamic and futuristic architecture to marvel at.

Geography

Kazakhstan is a landlocked, transcontinental country whose territory covers an area equivalent to the whole of Western Europe. The landscape stretches from the mountainous, populated south eastern regions to the energy-rich lowlands of the west and includes the industrialised north, with its Siberian climate and terrain, through the arid steppes of the centre. It is bordered by China, Kyrgyzstan, Russia, Turkmenistan, and Uzbekistan and occupies a similar strategic position in the history of the Silk Road—as a distant frontier where east met west. For eastbound Silk Road travellers on the direct central route and the longer but easier northern route, this region was the gateway to China.

Kazakhstan is by far the largest of the Central Asian republics, more than twice as big as the other four combined. From its mountainous south-eastern border with Kyrgyzstan and China the terrain transitions to deserts in the central and south-western part of the country and then to the world's largest dry steppe in the north—stretching from the Caspian Sea on the west to the Altai mountains in the east.

Early History

The history of Kazakhstan is intricately linked with the history of one of the world's greatest trading routes, the Silk Road. However Kazakhstan's story is noticeably different from that of Silk Road countries farther south and west. Although some regions were claimed by the ancient Persian Empire, there was little Persian influence on this distant frontier until much later in its history. Alexander the Great, notably called simply Alexander of Macedon locally, stopped short of these lands in his march of conquest, and the great wave of Islam came more slowly. The dominant force in the history of these regions has been the nomads from the north who swept southward across the steppes to raid, conquer, or settle. It is believed that the first domestication of the horse occurred on the steppes of Kazakhstan.

A nomadic, warlike people of Iranian origin, called the Scythians, finally gained control of the eastern Central Asian steppes and mountain valleys around 750 B.C. They roamed across the Kazakh steppe, with the centre of their culture in a region of south-eastern Kazakhstan and northern Kyrgyzstan called Zhetysu, literally "seven rivers" for the rivers that flow into Lake Balkhash. Maintaining their nomadic horse culture, the Scythians left no cities; however, they were expert goldsmiths as testified by beautiful jewellery and a full suit of golden armour found in a burial mound near the former Kazakh capital of Almaty.

From the west, Turkic people encroached on the Scythians around the 5th century A.D. while the Chinese to the east continued to monitor the land of Central Asia. A key moment in Kazakh history occurred in July 751 A.D., when the Chinese and Arab armies met on the Talas River near where it crosses the modern border of Kyrgyzstan and Kazakhstan. This was the only direct military contact between these two great Silk Road powers. A Chinese source estimated the Arab force as 200,000 soldiers—probably an exaggeration. The estimate of the Chinese force was more accurate: 10,000 Tang soldiers, 20,000 Turkic Karluk mercenaries from what is now eastern Kazakhstan, and an unknown number of Sogdians, who had resisted the Islamic onslaught.

The battle turned when the Karluks and Sogdians changed sides, perhaps seeing the inevitable outcome. In disarray the Chinese fled east of the Tien Shan with what was left of their army; of the 10,000 Tang soldiers, only 2,000 returned to China. For a time, the Chinese maintained their influence in the region, but by the end of the 8th century they were gone and did not cross the Tien Shan again for almost a thousand years.

Despite their connection on the Silk Road, the cities of Kazakhstan were slower to accept the Islamic religion as it swept up from the southern countries. The turning point came in 999 A.D. when a confederacy of Turkic tribes called the Karakhanids conquered much of Transoxiana, the area to the north and east of the Oxus River (today called the Amu Darya). The Karakhanids were devout Muslims, they came from the steppes of Kazakhstan and centred their empire in the east.

Located on a large oasis at the junction of routes leading to China, Persia, and the Eurasian steppes, Otrar was among the great Silk Road cities, but became the target for Mongolian revenge following the city's governor ordering an attack on a passing Mongolian trading caravan. In 1219 A.D., Genghis Khan led an army of between 100,000 and 200,000 warriors through Kazakhstan towards the heart of the Silk Road. While Genghis Khan orchestrated the destruction of Bukhara, an army led by two of his sons laid siege to Otrar, a new military technique that the Mongols had learned from the Chinese. After six months, they destroyed the city and slaughtered all its inhabitants. The governor was brutally killed by having molten silver poured into his eyes and ears. Although Genghis Khan had originally intended only to trade with the West, this marked the beginning of the westward invasions that would wreak destruction all along the Silk Road. As the 12th century Persian historian Ata-Malik Juvaini wrote, the injudicious action of the governor of Otrar had not only destroyed a caravan but "laid waste a whole world."

Unlike many cities destroyed by the Mongols, Otrar recovered and was once again a thriving trading centre by the mid 13th century. In the late 14th century, it became part of the empire of Uzbek conqueror Tamerlane, who died there in 1405 while gathering troops for an invasion of China. Today, Otrar is an archaeological site where the ruins reveal a well-organized, densely populated trading city in the transitional zone between nomads of the northern steppe and sedentary populations of the south.

The northern Silk Road route led from the city of Tashkent to Shymkent in southern Kazakhstan. There the road forked, with one branch leading to the northwest up the Syr Darya River toward the steppes and the other heading eastwards to China. Shymkent was founded in the 12th century as a caravanserai to protect the nearby city of Sayram, a trading centre believed to be 3,000 years old. Although a caravanserai was primarily a place for merchants to rest and trade, it could also serve as a fortification. In time Shymkent developed into a thriving market in its own right, where nomadic tribes came to trade with the farming and urban people. Although destroyed several times in the past, beginning with the invasion of Genghis Kahn, Shymkent today is one of the largest cities in modern Kazakhstan with a population of around 700,000.

From Shymkent, the route to China led to Talas on the Talas River, near the site of the Battle of Talas. Dating back to a fort built in the first century B.C., Talas emerged as a major fortified city on the Silk Road in the 6th century A.D. With abundant water from the river and fertile soil it became the centre of a city-state that fell under the domain of various powers, similar to many Silk Road cities. Like Shymkent it survived the Mongol invasion to become a large modern metropolis, called Taraz today.

Russian & Soviet Kazakhstan

From 1465 until 1731 Kazakhstan was governed by a poorly unified Kazakh Khanate made up of 3 key hordes, the Great jüz, Middle jüz, and Little jüz, who had to agree to the appointment of a Khan to lead them. Whilst this khanate brought together Kazakhstan's first rule of law, in 1731 there was no strong leader that emerged and one by one the regions of Kazakhstan became incorporated into the Russian Empire, whose traders and soldiers had already begun to appear on the north-western edge of Kazakh territory, building forts that eventually became the cities of Uralsk and Atyrau.

Following this "Great Retreat," the Russians began to colonise the region, despite numerous uprisings and wars in the 19th century that slowed progress. In 1863, the Russian Empire elaborated a new imperial policy, allowing it to annex "troublesome" areas on the empire's borders. This policy quickly led to the Russian conquest of the rest of Central Asia and the creation of administrative districts that destroyed much of the traditional Kazakh economy and was the death knell for nomadic life and its people, who were prohibited from driving their herds and flocks across the steppes.

The completion, in 1906, of the Trans-Aral Railway between Orenburg and Tashkent further facilitated trade and transport that was Russian led with Russian farms beginning to put immense pressure on the land and its precious water resources. Despite many Kazakhs joining the general Central Asian Revolt against conscription in to the Russian imperial army during the First World War in 1916, little damage could be done to the Russian power that brutally suppressed the revolt, killing thousands of Kazakhs. It was clear that Soviet rule was here to stay at the expense of the Kazakh people.

Even in Silk Road times, the downstream flow of the Syr Darya and Amu Darya rivers was greatly impacted by irrigation and other human needs, but when major Soviet irrigation projects began in the early 1960s they turned the Aral Sea into an ecological disaster that is one of the Soviet legacies today's leaders of Kazakhstan and Uzbekistan have to face. By 2007, the sea had shrunk to 10% of its normal size, divided into northern and southern parts. Fortunately, the northern part has begun to recover slightly due to a large dam built by Kazakhstan from its oil revenues.

Kazakhstan Today

With the dissolution of the Soviet Union, on 16th December 1991, Kazakhstan adopted the Constitutional Law on the independence of the Republic of Kazakhstan and broke free from Russian rule. The country's communist era leader, Nursultan Nazarbayev, became its first president and has ruled for more than two decades. Although he certainly doesn't encourage opposition, he has quickly managed to forge a peaceful, multiethnic nation that has kept him largely popular with his people.

Soon after independence, a two-chamber Parliament was established and a judicial system put in place alongside the determination of a new capital, Astana, taking the reins from Almaty to the south. Fundamental national legislation was passed on the economy, social security and the armed forces that has helped radically transform the Kazakh economy into an integrated world economy, gaining significant foreign investment.

While it is impossible to ignore the vast natural resource wealth that the oil and gas industry in Kazakhstan is bringing, the country boasts 99 of the 116 elements in the periodic table of elements in mined and mineable reserves providing it with a future of potential natural wealth that its neighbours eye jealously. It has also developed enough farm and pastureland to meet the immediate needs of its growing population of nearly 15 million, of whom nearly two thirds are Kazakhs.

The Kazakh people are fiercely proud of their tradition and heritage. This nomadic heritage is still heavily reflected in Kazakhstan, where traditional yurts—moveable, felt-covered homes—can be seen on the steppes and in mountain valleys. The nomads were people of the horse, and this heritage remains in the national cuisines, with horsemeat and mare's milk added to the traditional mutton and sheep's milk of other Central Asian countries (Camel's milk is also popular). Traditional sports of the steppe are still practiced as well. Hunting with golden eagles dates back thousands of years, as testified by Bronze Age petroglyphs and the discovery of a golden eagle in an ancient tomb in western Kazakhstan. The closely guarded secrets of the berkutchi (eagle hunter) are passed from father to son. Today, the Syugaty Valley, 150 kilometres east of Almaty, is the centre of Kazakh eagle hunting.

How to Use this Book

It is better to see something once, by experiencing, driving and touching it perhaps, than to hear about it a hundred times. However, in the case of Kazakhstan, this famous saying is only half right, because even hearing about Kazakhstan will likely have been a rare experience for many. If you have just bought this book, or are considering its purchase, then try and buy it together with a flight ticket and go to the centre of the Eurasian continent for yourself.

If you are already in Kazakhstan, then begin to read and consider it paragraph-by-paragraph, experience by experience. It goes without saying that it will take quite a lot time to experience everything that Kazakhstan has to offer (one glance at the map is enough to understand why). So, do not be discouraged if after a very intensive month or so in Kazakhstan, you have hardly experienced even a quarter of the feelings, emotions, places or senses described in these paragraphs. Just come back again and keep discovering the country. And even when the time comes that you are able to say that you have visited all 100 experiences of Kazakhstan in this book, you should not think that there is nothing more to experience in this amazing country. Believe us; we are ready to create another book of 100 experiences, because Kazakhstan is so large and diverse that there are at least another hundred experiences that are no less exciting and rich in surprises and your visit to Kazakhstan may just unveil a few more not captured here.

So, go ahead and find out what Kazakhstan is all about!

Astana

ASTANA

Astana is possibly one of the fastest-changing cities in the world: if you leave Astana for just a month, on your return you will see changes that would have taken years in other cities. Everything is new: the streets and houses, statues and squares, quays and bridges. The Left Bank, the new administrative and business centre, is where most of the changes are happening and the main attraction point for tourists. Many world-famous architects have contributed: Kisho Kurokawa, Norman Foster and Manfredi Nicoletti are among them. Akorda, Khan-Shatyr, Bayterek, Hazret-Sultan, Pyramide and the House of Ministries are just a few of the sights. Although Astana is mainly a modern city, some traces of it's distant past can be seen there as well. Within the city limits you can the find ruins of Bozok, a medieval settlement. As with any other big and developing city, Astana can be called the city of contrasts, because old, crumbling houses can neighbour modern and luxurious buildings. It is a matter of time, of course, before these disappear.

ISHYM RIVER

For its dry and shallow expanses, in the central part of the country, the River Ishim (in Kazakh, Yesil) looks really impressive. In Astana the riverbed has been widened and its banks are encased in granite that gleams in the sun. Ishim's riverside is a popular place among city dwellers and visitors to take a stroll in the evening or go jogging in the morning. One can admire this peaceful scene by sitting in a white fretted arbor on the high bank. You can also use the services of boatmen and discover Astana from aboard. Today, the river is a border between the old and quite simple Right Bank and the new and modern Left Bank, literally between provincial past and new capital gloss. Although, in the area of Akorda and Pyramid, you understand which future is waiting for the whole city very soon: here both the Left Bank and Right Bank are built-up in a modern and original way.

PALACE OF PEACE AND RECONCILIATION

They also call it the Palace of Peace and Accord. But, to be honest, nobody uses this term. Locals know it simply as Pyramid (because it has the shape of a pyramid). Situated on the Right Bank of Astana, just opposite the presidential residence, Akorda, the 62 metre high Pyramid is one of the most remarkable landmarks of the city. Like a number of other famous structures of Astana, the Pyramid was designed by the famous British architect, Norman Foster. Four sides of the Pyramid are oriented to the face the four sides of the world, this serves as a symbol of friendship, unity, peace and tolerance, which Kazakhstan adheres to. Actually, the Pyramid was built to host regular congresses of leaders of world and traditional religions. But it also has other facilities, including exhibition and conference halls, a huge opera hall, the International Centre of Cultures and Religions and the Academy of the Turkic World. "Besik" Hall, the lightest and the highest part of the Pyramide, is the place, where religious leaders used to meet during the congresses.

HAZRET SULTAN MOSQUE

Situated on the Right Bank of Astana, near the US embassy, Kazakh Yel monument and the Pyramid, Astana's main mosque is built of white marble and towers impressively at 77 metres. The name of the mosque, Hazret Sultan, reminds us of the most widespread title of saint sufi Khodja Akhmed Yassavi and, surprisingly, is a part of the Kazakh president's full name. Only since July 2012 has Hazret Sultan taken top spot from Nur-Astana mosque that was previously the main mosque and became the biggest mosque in Central Asia. Up to ten thousand people can pray in its huge territory (of more than 11 hectares) at the same time. From some angles, the Hazret Sultan looks so impressive, that the Pyramid (not a small structure itself) suddenly seems smaller and less stunning. There were even rumors that the National Geographic Channel shot an episode of its Mega Structures documentary about Hazret Sultan, but nobody has seen it yet. Who knows, great structures always attract great rumors.

AKORDA

This building, often carelessly referred to as the "White House of Kazakhstan", is very different in size and proportion to the residence of the U.S. president, but it is the palace and main residence of the First President of Kazakhstan. You will probably not be lucky enough to see inside of this "holy" edifice: Tours of the residence of the Kazakh president for tourists do not happen at all (except for the virtual tour on the official website). So to enjoy the magnificently pompous architecture you must remain on the outside and at a distance. The president has lived here since late 2004, which was when the new Astana residence was officially presented to the public.

Akorda is Kazakh for, "the white headquarter". This was the name of one of the "khanates" formed after the collapse of the famous Golden Horde, which was ruled by the descendants of Juchi, the eldest son of Genghis Khan, the ancestor of the future Kazakh rulers. Akorda is often seen as the core of the modern state of Kazakhstan with the official explanation for the name being that the white colour in the Turkic tradition simply means holiness, goodness, and prosperity.

6

BAITEREK

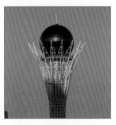

Baiterek is one of the original objects symbolising the new capital, and among the most mentioned and replicated on souvenir products. Baiterek Tower has for many years, been the defining symbol of Kazakhstan. Rising to a circular viewing platform from which there is a spectacular view of the new part of Astana, the "Left Bank" it is a must-see part of a visit to Astana. Baiterek has been "implanted" so deeply in the minds of the people, that it in many cities and villages it has been replicated. Do not be surprised, if you see many small and medium "Baitereks" in central areas of villages/towns during your trip to Kazakhstan.

According to popular legend, Baiterek - is the magical "tree of life", found by a hero of a number of Kazakh tales, Yer-Tostik, after a long journey. According to legend, a magic bird, Samruk, every year lays a golden egg in the branches of the tree, and all the dreams and desires of people are hidden in this egg. At 97 metres tall, the tower represents a stylized tree crowned with a huge golden dome representing this egg, which is 22 metres in diameter. One of the favourite pastimes for visitors to Baiterek is placing their hands next to the metallic impression of the palm of the first Kazakh President - Nursultan Nazarbayev, which is located in the panoramic Tower Hall. They also make wishes - and it is said that these wishes will come true...

KHAN SHATYR

Khan Shatyr (in Kazakh - "Khan's Tent") is another dramatic creation of the famous British architect, Norman Foster, that has already become one of the symbols of the Kazakh capital. A huge tent-shaped structure, whose spire rises to 152 meters, it is the largest of its kind across the globe. Khan Shatyr is located at the end of the "Millennium Axis", the central architectural component of the Left Bank of Astana, on the opposite side of which is the presidential residence, Akorda.

Foster, who designed the building, was planning to create an atmosphere of comfort and relaxation from everyday life and the outside world, including extreme weather conditions - very fitting for Astana's unique and, at times, severe climate. Khan Shatyr is the largest shopping and entertainment centre in Kazakhstan. In addition to boutiques, restaurants and movie theatres, there is also something quite unexpected - a beach resort with a truly tropical climate (it is always 35 degrees Celsius). Located here are corresponding tropical plants, sun loungers and parasols, as well as a heated sandy beach from the Maldives and warm water in pools with wave machines.

EXPO 2017

The Kazakh capital, Astana, will provide a grand stage when it hosts EXPO-2017 after winning its candidacy bid in 2013, beating the city of Liege in Belgium. Under the general theme of "Energy for the Future" the event will showcase the most notable achievements of mankind in the development of green energy. The country expects more than 5 million people from 100 countries and dozens of international organisations to visit. The numbers will dwarf the current population of Astana, who number just 758,000 people. EXPO-2017 will give Astana new attractions and, given the city's high number of already eye-catching buildings and architectural marvels, you can expect the skyline to boast something equally spectacular. Previous exhibitions have left iconic legacies such as the world-famous Crystal Palace built in London's Hyde Park in 1851 or engineer Gustav Eiffel's tower built in Paris for EXPO-1889. 113 hectares of land for the construction of the future Expo Centre has already been selected and promises to have a legacy of facilities and housing that will be of great benefit to the city and future generations of visitors.

Returning to the main theme of "Energy for the Future," Kazakh government policy aims to increase the share of renewable energy sources to 11% by 2030 and to show its commitment to such a target, the exhibition area in Astana will have its energy needs provided for solely by renewable energy sources, presenting a "City of the Future" for the world to see and perhaps aspire to. Book your ticket now, to avoid disappointment!

AIR ASTANA

Air Astana is quietly revolutionizing air travel to and within the vast and mysterious lands that make up Central Asia. From its base in Kazakhstan its modern fleet and award winning service are reviving the best traditions of the old Silk Road. Air Astana now ranks amongst the world's best airlines for passenger service. Since its inception on 15th May 2002, the airline's network has expanded to reach more than 60 international and domestic destinations. Air Astana became the first carrier from the Russia/CIS/Eastern Europe region to be awarded the prestigious 4-Star rating by Skytrax World Airline Awards and was also named The Best Airline in Central and South Asia. Air Astana currently operates the youngest fleet on the globe consisting of Boeing 767, Boeing 757, Airbus A319, Airbus A320, Airbus A321 and Embraer 190 aircraft. Friendly and professional cabin crew are delighted to provide you with the highest standards of service excellence always delivered "from the Heart of Eurasia". This guarantees you a warm welcome, and service that makes you feel at home the whole time you are on board with Air Astana.

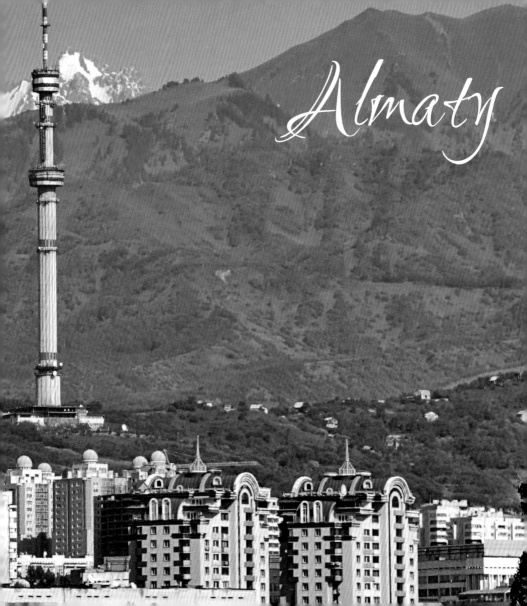

Almaty

ALMATY

Population is 1.5 million - Almaty is the former capital of Kazakhstan. It is already more than 15 years since the capital has been moved from mild and soft climate of North Tian-Shan into the cold and windy prairie of Central Kazakhstan. In spite of everything, Almaty is still the biggest city in the country and is the main commercial, financial, scientific and educational centre. Almaty is also the place where the majority of tourists come. The city has always been a good starting point for further journeys and is often included in the itinerary of many expeditions since the 19th century, whether it be Nikolay Przhevalsky and Peter Semenov-Tienshansky, or Ewan MacGregor and Charley Boorman. Explore the historical center with its merchant houses and old churches, visit one of its bazaars, go to Koktobe and Medeo, take a stroll along Almaty Arbat and fling yourself into the local nightlife.

GREEN BAZAAR / MARKET

Any Kazakh market is a bustle of people, goods, sounds and smells. Although it is difficult to find a real oriental bazaar here (as everything is usually quite modern), originality and exoticism, however, can be located. Almost any foreigner will want to spend a couple of hours at one of the local bazaars, as a visit tends to be quite memorable. The Green Bazaar in Almaty definitely tops the list as Almaty's prime attraction, however there is also the Central Kolkhoz Market (this was its official name in Soviet times) where, apart from fruits and vegetables, you can buy dairy products, honey, grains, spices, nuts, sweets, ready-made salads, clothing, houseware, construction materials and souvenirs, of course. The Green Bazaar is especially famous for meat of all kinds and various meat products that are really popular among Kazakh people: kazy, zhaya, karta, shuzhyk, etc. Unfortunately, nowadays it is officially prohibited to take photos inside Green Bazaar: just one of the strange Soviet-style rules, which Kazakhstan remains full of.

MUSEUM OF FOLK MUSIC INSTRUMENTS

Have you ever heard the names like Konyrau, Sazgen, Zhetigen, Asatayak, no? Then come to the museum and show to your children the folk musical instruments that the museum has to offer. You will be impressed by the new updated and renovated exposition.

For adults and children there is thematic excursion programs, master-classes on playing folk instruments and participation in theatrical performance and concert of the ethno-folk group "Turan".

The museum offers its halls for conducting children's birthday parties. Let your kids not only play with their favorite cartoon heroes, but also commit together with them an entertaining journey into the world of culture and music of their ancestors.

Also the cozy Concert Hall of the museum provides a platform for private concerts, weddings, celebrations and corporate events, national ceremonies, fashion shows, as well as seminars and trainings. There is a lecture hall with subscription programs and special projects for children.

ALMATY ARBAT

Almaty Arbat is a popular destination for rock fans, and in the evenings it is often possible to observe their gatherings for parties. This tree-lined pedestrian street is the first place any aspiring musician comes to busk. It is a favourite place for many groups in Almaty, and other unofficial events such as flash mobs, often utilise this venue. In Arbat, you can buy or just browse the works of local artists and photographers, as well as become a "hero" or a picture of professional photography.

Those who prefer to find art without a tourist bias can find a genuine piece of modern art in the Tengri-Umai gallery, which is located in one of the Soviet towers on the south side of the Arbat. For those who seek a genuine modern Kazakh atmosphere, it is also an ideal place catching up on life's gossip, sitting on a bench and watching the world go by, before having dinner at one of the romantic outdoor cafes, which are also abundant in Arbat.

KOKTOBE

Koktobe ("Green Hill"), a small hill bordering the south-eastern side of the Almaty metropolis. It is the most popular viewing area of the city, which is particularly spectacular during sunset and at night. The landscape stretches from Koktobe towards the snow-capped peaks of the Trans-Ili Alatau. Koktobe is also a very popular recreation destination. There are souvenir shops, rides, a petting zoo, restaurants, national cuisine and numerous cafes that allow you to combine culinary pleasures with cultural experiences. And the greatest surprise? A monument to the Beatles!

There is powerful TV tower on the top of Koktobe, some 372 metres tall, which is one of the trademarks of the city (although not a classic view, the panorama with a view of the TV tower is one of the most classic landscapes of Almaty), and another example of seismic resistance. The most interesting way to get to Koktobe is via a cable car that starts near the Palace of the Republic. During the 6 minute journey, you can enjoy the urban landscape with a bird's eye view.

MEDEO

Medeo, located in the Small Almaty Gorge, south-east of the centre of Almaty, became known throughout the world when it was built in 1972 as part of an alpine winter sports complex which sits about 1690 metres above sea level. The ice rink, with an area of 10.5 thousand square meters, is one of best top places to host international competitions in speed skating, hockey, and figure skating. Quite by chance, the strongest skaters of the world have set over 120 world records at Medeo.

Fortunately, the ice rink is open not only for professionals but also for those who want to skate for pleasure, and from November to March this is one of the activities available. The site has a mild climate and good infrastructure for recreation. It has become one of the first places in the outskirts of Almaty to which guests of the city are brought. Another attraction is the Medeo mud dam, which you can climb up by walking up the long "ladder of health," consisting of 837 steps. From the top you can enjoy a stunning view of the beginning the Northern Tien Shan's mountain peaks.

SHYMBULAK

The slopes of the ski resort Shymbulak (or Chimbulak) have been famous since the times of the Soviet Union. In 1954, 25 kilometres from Almaty, the resort opened its facilities for skiers. Shymbulak became one of the main training bases for Soviet skiers and its slopes repeatedly held Union and republican championships.

Shymbulak's topography means the ski slopes have a height difference of about 1000 metres. Its highest point, Talgar Pass, is 3,180 metres above sea level, while the base station is located at 2,260 metres. The ski run down from the top of Talgar Pass is 3.5 kilometres, with an average width of 25 metres and a slope of 11° - 29°. These parameters allow athletes to build up quite a speed over the course. The Shymbulak season lasts from mid-November to late March. You can access the base station by using the modern gondola that starts from the Medeo. There are 3 ski lifts from the resort that enable you to get to Talgar Pass. A snowboard park provides snowboarders the chance to show off their tricks. Equipment rental, including skis, snowboards and sleighs, can be found at the 4 star Shymbulak Hotel.

ZENKOV CATHEDRAL

The Holy Ascension Orthodox Cathedral is, deservedly, considered by many as the most interesting architectural monument of Almaty. The wooden building, rising some 56 meters, was built in the early 20th century, as project of architect S. Tropaevsky by the engineer Andrey Zenkov. The uniqueness of the building was manifested by the fact that it was able to withstand one of the strongest earthquakes experienced by the city at the end of 1910, when almost all of Almaty was destroyed. Remarkably, the only damage suffered by the cathedral was a bent cross on one of its domes. During the Soviet period, the building housed the Central Museum of the Kazakh Soviet Socialist Republic, then it became a concert and exhibition hall, and in 1995, it was returned to believers. After its successful restoration as an elegant cathedral, it now lies at the centre of the 28 Guardsmen Park. This is a very symbolic place, dedicated to the heroes of World War II – the 316 guardsmen of an Infantry Division formed in Almaty, who in the winter of 1941, during the Battle of Moscow, held back the enemy forces but died heroically in battle.

Country

AKTAU MOUNTAINS

The Aktau Mountains ("white mountains" in Kazakh), are located in the eastern part of the Altyn-Emel national park. Contrary to their name, these ancient mountains are not really white. They can be purple, brown, green, blue, or any other colour. Some of them do, however, become a dazzling white but only in the direct rays of the midday sun. In these mountains, there are many manmade architectural relics. Watchtowers, colonnades, and fortress walls of a medieval town can be made out, the once sharp edges of their walls abraded over many centuries. This splendour, which does need a little imagination, is the product of time and the unpredictable outcome of the wind, and rain.

AKSU RIVER CANYON

Aksu Canyon is one of the most spectacular places of Aksu-Zhabagly, the oldest protected area in Kazakhstan, founded in 1926 in the mountains of Western Tien Shan. Aksu is one of the largest and deepest canyons in Central Asia. Its depth ranges from 300 to 500 metres, while its width spans across 800 metres with a length of more than 30 kilometres. The descent into the canyon is quite complex and steep banks make it impassable in some areas. The sun-warmed rocks and river Aksu provide humidity and create the microclimate of a natural greenhouse in the canyon. The upshot of this is that there are some ancestral plants from bygone eras such as horsetails and ferns. When visiting, take a deep breath and inhale the incomparable flavour of the long-boled junipers. From April to June the gorge is a magnet for botanists from all over the world, because there are many flowering plants typical for Aksu-Zhabagly: Greig and Kaufmann Tulips, *Eremurus lactiflorus*, Karatausky onions, *scilla puschkinoides*, and a variety of wild fruit trees including apples, almonds, pears and cherries.

ASSY PLATEAU

Assy plateau is known for being the place where, in summer, you can be guaranteed to encounter the shepherds with their flocks of sheep and herds of horses, as well as seeing their yurts. These alpine meadows have been used since ancient times as "zhailau", which translates in English to the summer pastures. You can get a sense of what it might be like to live as a Kazakh herder on this mountainous plateau, situated at an altitude of 2800-3200 metres above sea level in the eastern part of the Trans-Ili Alatau. The most common impression visitors have when they look at the local scenery is the scale of its vastness and space. Giant green meadows stretch out ahead, the white yurts are dotted into the scene and animals graze peacefully surrounded by snow-capped peaks, which provide the perfect backdrop for this beauty. Such is the breadth of the scene that it is difficult to capture all the detail in one shot.

In the vicinity are Saki mounds, Turkic stone sculptures and rock paintings from different periods that have provided archaeologists and historians much information on nomadic life and culture. In the south-western part of the plateau is an astrophysical observatory for star-gazing enthusiasts.

BOZJIRA

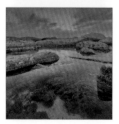

The most remote area from human civilisation in Kazakhstan is reserved for a part of Ustyurt that contains several hundred kilometres of eroded chalky valleys some 300 meters high that form a plateau. It is the habitat of the Ustyurt mouflon, Turkmen owl, honey badger and other rare desert animals. Reaching Ustyurt is complicated as there are no roads and the lunar landscapes require sturdy off-road vehicles. The special thrill of Ustyurt is Bozjira, two limestone "tusks", that are best observed from a nearby hill. White shades of limestone colour the entire valley with a snow-like effect. The unending maze of towers, canyons and architectural forms make for an easy location to get lost in and show just how strong nature can be in shaping the planet.

BORDER OF EUROPE AND ASIA

With recent discoveries of Russian geographers, the border of Europe and Asia in Kazakhstan has recently "moved" further to the east from its original location, thus making Kazakhstan a "more European" country than was previously thought.

Many consider these studies rather absurd (and pointless) and not recognised by the international geographical community, so we will continue to stick to the existing definition that has been in place for several centuries. This places the boundary between Europe and Asia in the northern Caspian region that runs along the Ural River. Accordingly, we will assume that being in Atyrau and going from the left bank of the Ural River to the right, or vice versa, will not only move you from one side of town to the other, but also will move you between the two parts of the world - Europe and Asia respectively. To play such a game is quite fun, especially as there are special pavilions on both sides of the bridge with inscriptions for Europe and Asia. Naturally these are popular places to pose for a picture.

BURKHAN BULAK

Burkhan Bulak, the highest waterfall in Central Asia, is located in the spurs of Jungar Alatau, in the south-east of Kazakhstan. Situated in a picturesque valley of the river Kora, the waterfall precipitates gallons of icy water from a height of 112 metres. The name of the waterfall suggests that this place has long been sacred for the mountain people because "Burkhan" in Mongolian means "Buddha". That's why many people think that somewhere in the surrounding mountains, not far from the waterfall, there was an image of Buddha. Some people still believe it exists, hidden from sight by the lush vegetation. To experience the true magic of the falling water, you can climb a little higher along the path that clings to the right hand side of the cliff and witness several multi-coloured rainbows shimmering in the mist of the spray.

CHARYN CANYON

It is often said that the Charyn (Sharyn) Canyon of Kazakhstan is a miniature version Colorado's famous Grand Canyon. This national park, located along the river Charyn (Sharyn), which is one of the tributaries of the river Ili, is among the most popular and most visited places in the country. But unlike its bigger brother in the United States, this is not the Wild West, but the Wild East. Its takes some adventure to get as far as the canyon though if coming from Almaty. Charyn Canyon is located on the border with China, some 200 kilometres from Almaty, and is accessible only with your own transport and over very poor roads. However, it is worth the uncomfortable ride to experience Kazakhstan's "Grand Canyon", stretching for 154 kilometres. Visitors are rewarded with exceptionally intricate canyon arches and caves up to 300 metres high, surrounded by steep slopes and jagged columns. These unusual rock formations, created by nature over thousands of years, are all too reminiscent of fairy tales, which is why different parts of the canyon have been assigned poetic names such as the "Valley of Castles" (the most popular area of the canyon) and the "Gorge of Witches."

The rocky cliffs of red sandstone are always beautiful early in the morning, at dusk, and at night under the moonlight. It is particularly beautiful in the spring, when the desert blooms, in the hot summer, under the hum of cicadas, and in the fall when the old trees along the river drop their leaves into the river, turning it a frothy gold. In the winter the white snow creates a graceful contrast with the red rocks.

KARAGIYE DEPRESSION

In the western part of the Mangishlak plateau, about 50 kilometres from the city of Aktau, stretching for over 40 kilometres from north-west to south-east is one of the deepest depressions in the world. At its lowest point it is 132 metres below sea level. Karagiye, derived from Turkish, means "black mouth". The formation of the depression is believed to be associated with the leaching of salt from the rock, subsidence and karstic processes that took place on the coast of the Caspian Sea, giving rise to fissures and sinkholes. These processes continue today, as evidenced by the cliffs and escarpments dissected by broad and deeply eroded gorges. A few years ago scientists conducted research in Kazakhstan, discovering that an almost waterless Karagiye was a natural generator of rain clouds. Ascending air in the summer cools and forms many kilometres of rain clouds over the depression. This occurrence is confirmed by satellite images obtained from space. The basin also has the reputation as an abnormal site where it is possible to see unidentified flying objects or encounter other paranormal phenomena.

KIYN-KERISH

Kiyn-Kerish is located 30 kilometres from the shore of Lake Zaisan and is also known as "The City of Ghosts," "The City of the Dead," "Flaming Cliffs," and "Martian Landscape." Many epithets are used to describe this miracle of nature. In fact, Kiyn-Kerish was uncovered by erosion sediments of red, orange, and white tertiary clays, which, being washed by water and blown by the wind for thousands of years, formed this unique and quaint scenery. Trapped within the remaining sediment rocks of Kiyn-Kerish are the remains of ancient vertebrate fauna including rhinos, crocodiles, turtles, salamanders, and other inhabitants of sub-tropical forests, as well as flora such as prints of palm trees, magnolias, araucaria, ginkgo, sycamore, oak, elm and chestnut.

Some see ancient cities and fortresses in the cliffs; in the precipices of the walls and towers, some see ships and yurts. In addition, in the late afternoon, the cliffs of Kiyn-Kerish mostly resemble flames bursting in the wind. It is a surreal feeling to stand there amongst the strong heat that prevails in the tract coupled with virtually a complete absence of water and winds of immense power that dominate the desert plains.

KOK-ZHAILAU

The spacious alpine Kok-Zhailau meadows, located neatly between the Big and Small Almaty gorges have traditionally been a favourite year-round vacation destination for those Almaty residents who are not strangers to mountain hikes and picnics in the open air. By happy coincidence, Kok-Zhailau, until recently, was left untouched by construction aimed at "civilising the mountains" and remained virtually the last unspoiled piece of nature close to the city.

METEORITE CRATER ZHAMANSHIN

To the north-west of the Small Aral Sea, lies a site that is popular among geologists across the world. Approximately one million years ago, a huge meteorite fell there with such force that the energy released was the equivalent to the explosion of multiple nuclear bombs. Geological deposits, buried deep beneath the earth's surface, were suddenly brought up into the atmosphere in the tumultuous impact. The diameter of the crater, according to recent data, is about 13 miles, and its depth today is approximately 300 metres. Zhamanshin is a unique place where you can discover fossils of molluscs and corals right under your feet, as well as tektites – black or dark green glassy formations whose, origin has been the subject of much dispute among scientists for more than a century. Some believe that tektites are terrestrial rocks that melted again during the explosion; others lean towards an extra-terrestrial origin of these materials, suggesting that these substances are the components of a comet's nucleus. Chemically, tektites do not resemble any well-known terrestrial and extra-terrestrial materials. The debate continues.

PLATEAU AKTOLAGAI

This chalky white plateau protrudes from the earth a few hundred kilometres from the border of the Atyrau and Aktobe regions and in the northern extension of Ustyurt, once a seabed. The abundant fossilised remains of shellfish, corals, sea urchins, and other marine life that lived millions of years ago can be clearly seen there. The teeth of ancient sharks, bones of ichthyosaurs (giant marine reptiles) and dinosaurs, petrified trees and plants of unknown species that can be found today attest to an unparalleled diversity. Looking out over the area, it is hard to believe that life once thrived and developed here. Today Aktolagai impresses with its desolate landscape, where the wind whistles ferociously over the desert and saline lands. Amongst the picturesque view of the white rocky outcrop there is only a handful of vegetation that provides precious shade from the glaring sun. Those who visit this solitary place look for silence and space among the un-trodden paths of adventure.

SINGING DUNE

The Singing Dune, is a huge dune of fine golden sand situated in the steppes. It is the most popular attraction of the Altyn Emel national park and is a very rare natural monument rarely seen elsewhere in the world. Locals believe that the dune "sings" when something or someone moves on its surface, although this phenomenon is really more due to the vibration noise created by the shifting sands moving in the wind or as a result of force. The dry sand becomes like a series of electrified grains that shower down rapidly, moving and rubbing against each other.

In order to fully experience the "musical talents" of dune you need to walk to its crest and then jump and run quickly down the slope to the base. The more people that do this, the better the sound. Everyone describes it differently, some think it is a whistling or squeaking sound, others a booming roar or hum. Whatever you hear, the sand will get everywhere and remains there for days, in your shoes, clothes and hair as a "free souvenir". Each time it leaves your clothing it will crackle a little and evoke the memories of your trip to the Altyn-Emel's "singing" sand dune.

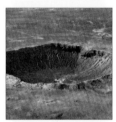

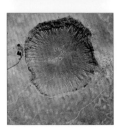

SHUNAK
METEORITE CRATER

40 kilometres to the west of the Moiynty railway station, in the south-eastern part of Qaraghandy Province, is one of the most interesting natural monuments of extra-terrestrial origin – the Shunak Meteorite Crater. The crater is believed to have formed about 12 million years ago as a result of the impact of a huge meteorite, which is thought to have obliterated all living creatures for several thousand kilometres. Shunak is 3100 metres in diameter (which is two and a half times the diameter of the famous Arizona crater in the U.S.) and 400 metres deep. Many believe that this is a mystical place with unusual powers, which brings all types of curious visitors to see it as well as its cousin, the Zhamanshin crater northeast of the Small Aral Sea.

SPHERICAL CONCRETIONS IN THE "VALLEY OF BALLS"

In the Mangystau region, surrounding the village of Shaiyr, the Sherkala mountain and the Zhingildi tract, there lie an astonishing number of bizarre stone balls scattered across the landscape. These spherical mysteries, which can be up to 3 metres in diameter, look like giant unexploded comets from another world or the cannon balls of giants. They are in fact the Earth's creation, although scientists have never agreed their age or true origin. These so-called concretions, probably 120-180 million years old, may have been derived from underwater deposits in the ancient Tethys Ocean, especially from clays or siliceous flows. In the deep water, a thin surface layer of sediment formed in an area of oxygen-bearing red clays before being compacted by subsequent sediment. In these layers iron and manganese minerals precipitated into the space between the sediment grains forming a cement, or crust. Over a long time these layers grew and gradually became spherical or ovoid in shape, sometimes incorporating the fossils of marine life that provides great paleontological and geological interest.

STEPPES OF SARY-ARKA

Ancient Kazakhs call this spacious area between the Ulytau Mountains in the West and Kalb Ridge in the East, "yellow ridge", in Kazakh, "Sary-Arka". Those who travel in the summer and discover these vast plains, with their intermittent low mountain massifs with forests and lakes, can easily understand this place's name. From the middle of July the silvery-green feather grass steppe under the generous sun turns into a solid golden yellow colour. Nomads with their flocks and herds have migrated to the mountains, to the green summer pastures. The Sary-Arka Steppe is the ideal place to unwind and give your soul some peace for those who spend their everyday lives in bustling cities, surrounded by walls, computers, cars, noise and smog. There are no such nuisances in the steppe – you meet only the wide blue sky, the wind, and at night, a starry sky that you will never forget.

The steppe is the only natural UNESCO World Heritage listed area in Kazakhstan at the present. The steppe and lakes of Sary-Arka expand across part of the Korgalzhyn and Naurzum reserves among others.

ZHUMBAKTAS AND OKZHETPES

Borovoye (in Kazakh - Burabai) is an oasis in the steppes north of the capital, which consists of several large and small lakes (including Lake Burabai), and low, forested mountains. This is a favourite resort of Astana residents who have been building extravagant houses to rest in, away from the hustle and bustle of the city. You can spend days just lying on the beaches and swimming in the lakes. Depending on your interests, you can go for a mountain walk and take in some fresh air or if looking something less strenuous, you can just bicycle on perfectly flat roads. Many enjoy simply doing nothing, enjoying the fresh air of the pine forest. Naturally the area has evolved into providing a mixture of business and leisure activities as well as a medical retreat for recuperation. All of this occurs with the stunning backdrop of the island of Zhumbaktas and the rocky mountain Okzhetpes prevailing over the local terrain.

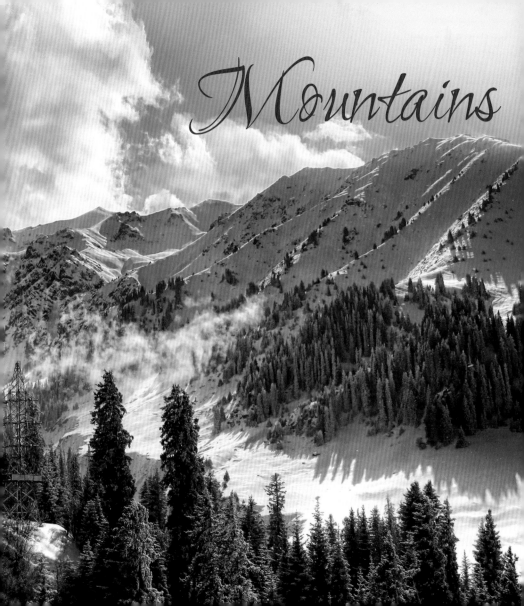

Mountains

KHAN-TENGRI

In the mountains of the Central Tien-Shan, on the border of three countries - Kazakhstan, Kyrgyzstan and China – lies the Tengri-Tag ridge, with its highest point the legendary and sacred mountain of Turks Khan-Tengri (6,995 m). It is the dream of many climbers.

The name is Mongolian and means "Lord of the sky". Kazakhs and Kyrgyz also commonly refer to it to as the "Kan Tau", which literally means "Bloody Mountain" because at sunset the upper part turns almost red. Mixed with the shadows from the clouds, the mountain creates the illusion of streams of scarlet blood flowing down its sides. The perfect pyramid that caps Khan-Tengri makes it look like the highest peak in the Tien Shan and for many years this was believed to be the case. Only in the 1950s was it proved that the height of Khan-Tengri Peak is 400 metres lower than Pik Pobedi (Victory Peak). The first explorers to summit the mountain were Mikhail Pogrebetskiy, Boris Tyurin and Franz Zauberer who ascended Khan-Tengri from the Kyrgyz south side on September 11, 1931.

BEKTAU-ATA

About 70 kilometres north of the city of Balkhash is one of the most remarkable places in North Balkhash – the mountain oasis Bektau-Ata, whose highest peak is a reference point for an expanse of land that is largely untouched by humans and full of natural diversity. The highest point of the mountains, the Bektau-Ata peak, reaches 1,214 metres above sea level, and its height from the top to bottom is about 600 metres.

Bektau-Ata is an un-erupted volcano, geologically known as a pluton, where sub-volcanic lava has hardened and formed a series of cracked dikes that permeate the mountain Over thousands of years, weathering processes have carved the granite into a series of true works of art – a series of bizarrely shaped rocks that people have given strange names to such as, "mushroom", "chest", "turtle" and "triple-tooth". On one of the slopes of the mountain range is a legendary cave with a spring that people believe has curative water. It is believed that the ancient Turks carried out sacrifices to the goddess of fertility here. To this day the cave is considered viviparous and childless women come here to seek help.

CENTRE OF KAZAKHSTAN

Ulytau (in Kazakh "the great mountain") is one of the great granite masses, which rise suddenly out of the expanses of the flat steppe. In the history of Eurasian nomads, this land has always occupied a special sacred role; some even consider this place "epicentre" of nomadic civilisation. A concentration of mausoleums, petroglyphs, caves, ancient cities and legendary stories create an environment that makes Ulytau the centre of Sary-Arka, and of the whole of Kazakhstan. In recent years, Ulytau was also awarded the complimentary title of "the cradle of the nation". Here Khans have been raised from birth and the headquarters of Kazakh rulers have been located since the earliest of times. The Ulytau mountains are in the geographic centre of Kazakhstan, as if to emphasise their significance. Just south of Ulytau village, the highly visible monument of Kazakhstan People's Unity attests to this importance.

BELUKHA

The Altai Mountains and its highest point - Mount Belukha - have attracted travellers from all over the world for many years. This eternally snow-capped mountain is a magnet for admirers, known as the gateway to the world of gods, the legendary Shambhala. Located on the border of Russia and Kazakhstan, crowning the Khatun Ridge, the eastern peak of Belukha rises above sea level to a height of 4506 metres. Symbolically, the mountain's two-headed peak resembles a saddle and many attribute this to the reason behind the special veneration of the mountains by ancient people. After all, Altai was the cradle of ancient nomads, who subsequently spread all over the Eurasian continent.

The most famous admirer of Belukha was the philosopher and artist Nicholas Roerich. Enchanted by the Altai mountains, Belukha, its mysteries, caves and meadows, Roerich depicted the surrounding landscape in his paintings, allowing the mountain range to become known across Russia and abroad. Despite this fame, the summit seemed insurmountable until 26th July 1914, when two brothers, Boris and Mikhail Tronovs, became the first to successfully ascend it.

SHERKALA MOUNTAIN

Sherkala Mountain, which is located near the Shayir settlement, is regarded as both a natural and historical landmark. It is a 300 metre high remnant of miraculous shapes, resulting from elevation of the land from the ocean depths. People say that the mountain resembles an inverted leech, yurt or sleeping lion in shape.

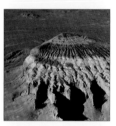

Sherkala means "tiger-city" in Farsi and there is a belief that the mountain has taken this nickname due to the bravery of its residents who live at the foot of the mountain. During enemy attacks, they went to a stronghold on the hill and defended from here. An ancient well at the top of the mountain has been found, which confirms this theory. There are also caves in the rock where most people are afraid to go because there is a belief that the last defenders of the mountain stronghold hid in these caves while retreating and have stayed there ever since.

Not far from the mountain, there are excavations of the ancient site of Kizil-Kala, which was the largest city and a caravanserai in the littoral lands of Caspian in the Middle Ages. It stood on a branch of the Silk Road that led to Astrakhan on the northern part of the Caspian Sea.

CLIMBING THE AKSORAN

The panorama from the top of Aksoran mountain immediately compensates for the hours that you need to make your way through the thorny bushes, as you climb to the top. The epithet "roof of the steppes", as used in recent years regarding Aksoran in newspapers and magazines, has become the second name of this mountain top in tourist itineraries (and is sometimes applied to the entire massif).

Aksoran is the highest point of the Kyzylarai Mountains and although its height of 1,565 metres is modest in relation to other mountains, the fact that it rises out of the flat steppe makes it appear a little surreal. From the top you can appreciate the immense area of the vast steppes that stretch out in front and then curve away in the distance, confirming that the Earth is, in fact, round.

Lakes

ALAKOL

Alakol, spread out a little east of Lake Balkhash, near the "Jungar Gates" and the border with China, is expected to be the jewel of a future tourist centre. This salt lake in a lunar landscape is located in the cleanest region of Kazakhstan; it is not affected by industrial and other human activities. Despite the fact that in winter the temperature frequently drops to 30 degrees below zero, this vast lake, 54 metres deep, enjoys summer temperatures of over 30 degrees Celsius. The water contains significant amounts of trace elements, which are believed to have healing properties that help bathers to get rid of various ailments. Small stony beaches provide perfect resting places on the banks of Alakol.

Within Alakol's area, in this area 20-30 kilometres from the shore, there are several islands, the largest and most important of which is the island Ulken Araltobe (also known as Stone). On this island the rare Alakol relict gull (Larus relictus) breeds. Access to the island is not open to all, however, as it is part of the territory of the Alakol Reserve.

AK-ZHAIYK RESERVE

This reserve, which is located at the place where the Ural River flows into the Caspian Sea, is one of a handful of global conservation areas providing a wetland habitat for migratory birds. The significance of the Ural River delta is, in particular, the fact that this area is an important area for migratory birds who fly the Siberia to East Africa route. Here, visitors will often see pink flamingos, Dalmatian pelicans, spoonbills, ibis, and other rare and endangered species of avifauna, not to mention the numerous ducks, geese, and swans. However, the Ural River delta is not only valuable for birds, it also hosts a unique and now endangered sturgeon species, the Russian beluga sturgeon, highly sought after in Moscow and the rest of the world for its buttery-flavoured caviar eggs. Finally, the reserve is also home to the Caspian seal, a species who, by its very existence, has shown links that prove the Caspian Sea was once part of the ancient Tethys Ocean that covered the area.

CAPE SHEKELMES

Lake Zaisan in East Kazakhstan is widely regarded as a mystical place. This is largely due to an interesting natural phenomenon: with the onset of darkness, melodious sounds over the water surface can be heard, like humming wires. The mysticism and antiquity of Zaisan can clearly be felt in Cape Shekelmes. Looking at its layered colours and surreal landscape, it is easy to imagine how dinosaurs and woolly mammoths roamed the banks of this lake.

It is believed that hundreds of millions of years ago a meteorite fell, turning the solid earth inside out and raising ancient rocks to the surface. The layered mountains, whose multi-coloured layers slant awkwardly, are considered by many to confirm this theory. You can collect your own souvenirs on the coast of Zaisan such as polished stones, whose layered design conveys a miniature characteristic of the local rocks and whose smooth surface is the result of thousands of years of action by the waves of the lake. But please do not take too many of these natural gifts with you; you should also think about those who will be here after you – a couple of photos is probably enough of a souvenir.

KOLSAI LAKES

Kolsai is a system of three lakes located in the mountains of the Northern Tien Shan, 300 kilometres away from Almaty. The lakes are a kind of "cascade", one after the other, in the huge mountain gorge of Kungei Alatau, surrounded by alpine meadows and pine forests. The highest of the lakes is at an altitude of about 2,700 metres above sea level. The usual tourist itinerary includes a visit to all three lakes, with access to the highest of these, which is close to the Sary-Bulak Pass. The Saty village, which is not far from the first Kolsai Lake, is one of the best examples of Kazakhstan's ecotourism development, based on engaging the local communities to open up to foreign visitors and share their unique perspective. The system of guesthouses, which was started about 10 years ago, is open to both foreign and Kazakh tourists improving the well-being of the local community and its individual members. The tour of the lakes and trails usually takes two to three days and it is possible to set up camp by the calming dark blue waters of the lake.

LAKE BALKHASH

To the southeast of Karaganda and north of Almaty, at the junction of the Karaganda and Almaty regions, sits Lake Balkhash, one of the largest lakes in the world (comprising approximately 18,000 square kilometres). The uniqueness of Balkhash is that half of it contains fresh water whilst the other half contains salt water. The eastern end is salty while the western parts are freshwater and the lakes are separated by a narrow strait, Uzin-Aral. The depth of Lake Balkhash does is just under 26 metres and it stretchesfor more than 600 kilometres. Unfortunately, the presence of the Balkhash Mining and Metallurgical Plant in the city means that only an area at considerable distance from the city, on the north shore of the lake, is suitable for visitors to relax. Away from the niose of the city and the roads, a trip to such a remote place will be remembered as a real adventure. One of the nicest places to stay is the secluded peninsula Baigabyl, located 140 km east of the city, in the saline part of the lake. The surrounding scenery is striking due to the purity of its water that glistens back at you with an invitingly pleasant turquoise colour.

LAKE INDER

The water in Lake Inder and the nearby caves and hollows in the northern Atyrau region - is brackish (salty) and therefore is believed to have healing properties. The lake is fed by 10 salt springs, from which the most beneficial to health is Aschybulak, located on the northeast coast. You can see numerous "baths" in which people take water and mud treatments. Often there are specimens of ancient fossils - sea urchins, shells and coral – that can be discovered In addition, a tour to the nearby Inderborsk mine, which is located at a depth of 300 metres, and has a length of 30 kilometres, will take you right under lake Inder into an underworld of salt production and mineral mining. Due to the sterility of air, impregnated with salts, staying in the mine also provides a healthy environment. Added to this, the multi-coloured walls of rock salt provide a quite incredible backdrop to one cave that has been converted into a glistening underground palace.

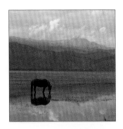

LAKE MARKAKOL

Markakol has been deemed the blue pearl of the Altai Mountains. Located at an altitude of 1,485 metres and surrounded by Kurchum ridge and Azutau ridge, it is the centre of the Markakol reserve. With an area of 455 square kilometres, its maximum depth reaches 27 metres. Ninety-five watercourses flow into the lake and only one full-flowing river, the Kaldzhir, flows out. The picturesque environment of Markakol, surrounded on all sides by luxuriant mountainous vegetation, is a good backdrop for both a relaxing or active holiday. Many have noted an amazing variety of colours and beauty unique to the lake. It can be blue or azure, grey or almost black, silver or greenish. Nature lovers especially enjoy watching the lake in the late afternoon when it takes on a golden hue as the sun sets over the horizon. Before you go, you need to keep in mind that the Lake Markakol district is the coldest place in Kazakhstan. Summers are warm, but never hot. Snow melts only at the beginning of May. The best time for a trip to Markakol is from the middle of August to the end of September.

LAKE SHAITANKOL

The Karkaraly Mountains are regarded as one of the most popular holiday destinations for the past few decades in Central Kazakhstan. In addition, the most amazing and beautiful of these destinations is Lake Shaitankol (or "Devil's Lake" in Kazakh). The lake is too cold to swim in and there is no sandy beach, but amidst its beauty there are also many ancient legends. Usually the legends tell of an unrequited love that ended tragically in or near the lake. Many people comment that you feel a certain mysterious and mystical atmosphere produced by the noise of the pine trees and precipitous cliffs nearby. Animals, in particular, exhibit odd behaviours as a result and can often be heard whining or are seen becoming strangely excited. Tourists rarely stay here for the night, and those who dare often return with stories of unusual things that occurred on the lake during the dark.

BIG ALMATY LAKE

The Eastern branch of the Big Almaty gorge, to the south from Almaty, leads the traveller to the Big Almaty Lake, surrounded by mountains covered with conifer forests. These are the Trans-Ili Alatau Mountains, with at an altitude of about 2500 metres above sea level. The panorama from the shores of the lake is charming with the distinct "Peak of the Soviets", the road to the Ozyorniy pass and the spurs of the Big Almaty Peak all reflecting in harmony with the deep turquoise colour of the lake.

Big Almaty Lake, or BAO, which is what Almaty residents call it, was formed about 10,000 years ago by the collapse of the land associated with tectonic movements. You can still see traces of faults and imagine the scale of the ancient catastrophe. In 1977 a devastating mudflow prompted an increase to the security defences of the city, including increasing the height of a natural dam on the Big Almaty Lake by 10 metres. Nowadays, there is a modest hotel of the Tien Shan Observatory next to the lake (formerly the State Sternberg Astronomical Institute, SAI), where, if you are lucky, can look at the starry sky through a telescope.

SUNSET ON THE CASPIAN SEA

The Caspian Sea is a sea in name only. Although it covers an area of 371,000 square kilometres and is salty, it is actually considered a lake, and the largest in the world at that. The lake inherited the word "sea" in its title from ancient times when it was once called the Southern Sea, then Hirkanian after Khvalynsky or Khazar. Its modern name was given to it by the Caspian tribes who used to live on its coasts as far back as the time of Christ's birth.

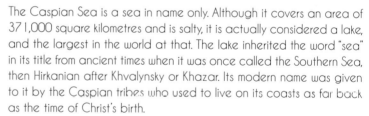

Anybody who stumbles across the Caspian Sea should enjoy the surf and sea breeze, with swimming usually possible between May and September without needing a wetsuit. And then after a hard day's activities you can watch the sun setting into its waves in the west with a cold drink from a dozen sites in the city of Aktau.

BLOSSOMING TULIPS

In the spring and summer, the steppes and foothills of Kazakhstan begin to bloom with all the colours of the rainbow, and the tulips are the reason. Thousands of tourists, eager to capture the tulips' bloom in their memories and photographs, are sent every year around this time into the fields. Tulips can be regarded as one of the main attractions of Kazakhstan. It is in fact the Kazakh wild tulips that have given rise to cultivars, grown for centuries in the Netherlands. Overall, there are 38 species of plants, 18 of which are categorised as endangered. You can arrange to see the different tulip blooms yourself from late April to June in different regions of Kazakhstan. In the Korgalzhyn reserve you can see Schrenk tulips, then to the south of Kazakhstan, in Aksu-Zhabagly and the botanical reserve, Berkara, are Greig tulips, Kaufman tulips and others. The Kolpakovsky Tulip can be found in the Ile-Alatau National Park and the open spaces of the National Park Altyn-Emel, while the virtually extinct Regel tulip, a unique and endemic species, is preserved only in the Chu-Ili Mountains. Beautiful as these flowers are, there is one strict request for the visitor: Please do not pick the flowers as this can harm the bulbs.

BIRD WATCHING

Many tourists come to Kazakhstan, not for its vast steppes or snowy peaks, nor to explore the everyday life of the local population, or for excursions to historic sites, but solely to spend a week or two in its wetlands in order to capture as many birds as possible in their memories and photographs. With 500 species of bird living in (or flying to) the territory of Kazakhstan the country is a haven for all types of birdwatchers who are sure to spot a variety of birds that arrive here for breeding, feeding, resting, or moulting. In places such as the Korgalzhyn reserve or Aksu-Zhabagly reserve, hundreds of bird watchers descend every year, armed with detectors, cameras with long lenses, large telescopes and binoculars, as well as a bit of patience. Although this is a bird's paradise, many often finish the trip also realising that Kazakhstan is an interesting country with a rich history and stunning landscapes.

CAMELS AND SHUBAT

Kazakh camels, classically two-humped and lanky, occur largely in the south of the country and in its western part. These are the desert and semi-desert regions. There are a few exceptions in the form of a camel farms that are found in the central part of Kazakhstan. Domestic camels, of course, are much smaller than horses, but they leave a mark in the hearts of travellers who visit Kazakhstan. The romantic image of a camel along the Silk Road is easy to capture as they often pose for the camera lens with great calmness. Camels are also remarkable for their Shubat – a fermented milk drink, a little fatter and thicker than mare's milk. It is unbelievably thirst-quenching on hot summer days.

GREATER FLAMINGOS

Korgalzhyn Reserve, rightly entered in the List of World Heritage Sites by UNESCO, is a unique ecosystem preserved in an almost natural state of the steppes with a variety of large and small saltwater and freshwater lakes. It is also notable that in the largest salt lake, Tengiz, nests a colony of common (or greater) flamingos (Phoenicopterus roseus). The wetlands of the reserve are the northernmost habitats of these species and are the largest in Central Asia. 20,000 pairs these elegant birds nest here. Flamingos can be seen at Lake Tengiz from early May to late September. For the winter, the birds migrate to warmer climes, mostly to the lakes in the Middle East (Southern Turkmenistan, Iran, Iraq, Egypt, Turkey, Afghanistan, and Pakistan).

Flamingo astonish with their simultaneous gracefulness and clumsiness, perched on fragile legs, "stilts". The fact that they live here, in the harsh expanses of the steppes of Kazakhstan, where storms prevail during winter and temperatures can reach as low as minus 40 degrees, should attract even those who are indifferent to seeing animals in their natural habitat.

RELICT TURANGA

Diversifolia Asiatic, also known as heterophyllous poplar (Populus Diversifolia) or Asian Poplar, appeared on earth in the Tertiary period, somewhere between the time when the dinosaurs died out, and the moment when the last ice age began. The characteristic feature of the tree, also known as Turanga, is that the leaves are very different in shape and size, depending on where they grow. They may be tapered, narrow and long, or broad and round. The Asian poplar, thanks to its strong root system submerged in the soil to a depth of 50 metres, is capable of pumping water from the sand and can survive in the harsh desert and semi-desert conditions present in Kazakhstan.

One of the best places to see Turanga is the Altyn-Emel national park, where it forms a large grove of trees. Turanga is also found in Charyn canyon and in northern Balkhash lakeside (lower reaches of the river Tokyrau), as well as a few other places in Kazakhstan, including the Kyzyl Kym, the lower reaches of the rivers Ural and Irgiz.

SAIGA

Sixty years ago thousands of Saiga antelope (Saiga Tatarica) herds migrated to the vast expanses of the Kazakh steppes. These small antelope, that appear more like a sheep on long legs, have distinctive flexible noses that look almost like the head of a vacuum cleaner! Due to their excellent adaptation to the harsh climate of the steppe, these types of animals have lived on Earth since the times of mammoths. However, the barbarous extermination, which began in the late 1890s, has put this species under great threat of extinction (for example, it is estimated that from the original population of half a million animals that once existed in central Kazakhstan, there were only a couple of thousand by 2003). In the end, the species was included in the IUCN Red List and included under protective status by the World Wildlife Fund. In Kazakhstan, the campaign to protect and increase the number of Saiga is making good progress, under the framework of the "Altyn Dala", overseen by the Kazakhstan Association of Biodiversity Conservation (ACBK). Now, the steppes of Kazakhstan are home to the greatest number of individuals - about 80% of the total global population. Three of its major population centres in Kazakhstan are Ural (West Kazakhstan), Ustyurt (Ustyurt) and the previously mentioned Betpak-dala (Central Kazakhstan), which is the largest. According to the latest reports by biologists, there are estimated to be approximately 60,000 Saiga in the steppes of Kazakhstan today.

STEPPE EAGLE

Sitting on the power lines along the roads, on the rocks and mountain peaks soaring above the steppe, Steppe Eagles can be found wherever there is sky and the wind is blowing. Perhaps that is why they bear their name, as they are a symbol of Kazakhstan's steppes. The Steppe Eagle is a rather large bird (with a wingspan of up to 190 centimetres), so it is hard not to notice, even against the background of the boundless steppes.

Often, when filming in Kazakhstan, film directors will start with a shot of this predator hovering over the steppe and seeking food. The image of the Steppe Eagle in Kazakhstan can be found everywhere - from confectionery to beer brands and even on the national flag of Kazakhstan.

HORSES

They used to say that Kazakhstan is a nation born in the saddle. The saying is very true, if we take into account the fact, that a horse for a nomad was simultaneously both their transport (personal and cargo) and food (in the form of meat and milk). The lives of man and horse were tightly bound. The character of the Kazakh horse was formed by its natural environment: it is not very tall, but very strong. Local horses are also notable for their resistance to the cold and their endurance. Being in Kazakhstan, a country that is home to the descendants of ancient nomads - the Scythians, Huns, Turks and Mongols - and not giving horse riding a try for yourself would be a great pity. Some people come here specifically to ride horses in the wilderness, feeling, albeit briefly, unrestricted and free. It is not surprising, because the feeling of boundless freedom is almost instantly experienced in the saddle. Maybe it is how our genetic memory works? In winter, horse riding is even more logical and practical, because the horse can reach places where cars cannot pass.

APPLES

It is an interesting fact, that Malus Sieversii, a wild apple, native to the mountains of Tien Shan, is considered the ancestor of the overwhelming majority of domesticated apple varieties. The apple is actually one of the main symbols of Almaty and even the name of the city derives from the Kazakh word for "apple" (alma). It's no accident: wild apple forests were abundant in Almaty's surroundings some time ago. The most famous sort of apples in Kazakhstan is Almaty Aport, which appeared in the second half of the 19th century as a result of crossing local Malus Sieversii with imported Aport from the Voronezh region of Russia. Almaty Aport is a very large type (it is not uncommon for them to grow as large as half a kilo in weight). There was a time when the Almaty foothills were rich with apples, but the situation is changing: it is not so easy to buy Aport these days. Apple gardens and forests have become the first victims of thoughtless building in Almaty's foothills and other areas. But far away from the big cities, in other sub-mountain regions, apples are still grown. For some farmers it is their main business. You might ask: why don't they produce cider in Kazakhstan? It's a good question and perhaps they should try!

SNOW LEOPARD

Snow leopard (its local name is "irbis" or "barys") can be fairly called one of the most popular brands of Kazakhstan. Irbis is depicted at the emblem of the main development plan of the country (it is almost used as an official symbol, because Kazakhstan itself is called "the central asian snow leopard"), it is the main part of the emblem of Almaty, it was a talisman of the Asian Olimpic games 2011, there is even a beer made in Almaty and called "Irbis". Look back and you will see, that the hat of the Golden Man of Issyk was decorated with golden images of snow leopards. So, this is the fact, that the Red listed big cat is (and always was) the symbol of high-usage here.

In Kazakhstan you can meet snow leopards in Tien Shan, Jungar Alatau, Saur-Tarbagatai and Altai mountains. The approximate population size of irbis in Kazakhstan is not very big at the moment (about 100-120 units) and poaching still takes place being a serious problem. One of the best places for meeting a snow leopard is Almaty nature reserve, situated south-east of Almaty. Meeting the big cat is definitely hard, as snow leopard is a very cautious animal. So, you should remember, that a good photo always needs a lot of time and a lot of patience.

People

BAIKONUR COSMODROME

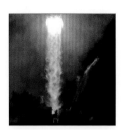

In the south of Kazakhstan, between Kyzylorda and the Small Aral Sea is one of the most advanced technical achievements in the world, the Baikonur Cosmodrome. On April 12 1961, the first manned flight into space was launched from this place. The spaceship used was called "Vostok" and was piloted by Soviet cosmonaut Yuri Gagarin. His journey lasted 1 hour 48 minutes and made a complete orbit of the planet.

Although at the time, Baikonur and the nearby city of Leninsk were "closed areas", today access to this place of technological miracles is relatively easy. Despite this, relatively few people come to see the present launches. Since the launch site is shared by both Russia and Kazakhstan, entering its territory requires the permission of both parties, which is not necessarily a quick process. Witnessing this stunning phenomenon – a rocket launch into space – remains a dream for many people. If you cannot obtain access to Baikonur personally, just watch the film by German director, Veit Helmer, titled "Baikonur" in which the inner workings of Baikonur are shown in great detail.

BERKUTCHI

People whose passion and profession is hunting with birds of prey, especially falcons *(Falco Cherrug)* and Golden Eagles can still be found in Kazakhstan. You could even say that this ancient craft is experiencing a renaissance, especially amongst wealthy hunters from abroad. Berkutchi not only hunt, they are also mentors of birds, taming them and instilling in them the necessary skills and habits. The Golden Eagle is a strong bird that can easily catch a fox, although it also hunts other birds and small animals. Today in Kazakhstan regular competitions are held among Berkutchis and these are a continuation or a reflection of the ancient custom of "salburyn" (mass group hunting during certain celebrations). Interestingly, many women are counted among professional Berkutchis.

DOMBRA

Some might say that the sound of the Kazakh Dombra instrument is too plaintive, and only sad thoughts may come to mind when running your fingers over its two strings. However, these days, the sounds and the tunes (which can be very energetic and even fun) are very strongly associated with the Kazakh culture. The Dombra is a long-necked lute that is most commonly found with two strings, although different regional variations sometimes have three. The Dombra has a flat pear-shaped triangular or quadrangular tapered body and neck with frets to aid the musician. Originally lamb or goat intestines were used as strings, but now it is replaced by more affordable and durable nylon. A special style of Kazakh folk art is connected with the Dombra called, "kuy" which is an improvised genre of music. Competitions reward the most talented is and quick-witted people with the instrument.

FELTING

Traditions of felting in Kazakhstan come from time immemorial. Ancient nomads understood that the fibres of sheep or camel wool, under the influence of hot water and steam can turn the material into a very solid and durable construction. Felt is used in carpets, blankets, clothes, and shoes. Unfortunately, modern Kazakhs have already forgotten many of the techniques, as Chinese industry, as it has done throughout the world, has made the process much easier and less labour-intensive. However, with the help of various educational projects, traditional skills are gradually resuming and reviving. Moreover, what is encouraging is that felt is not only being used to dazzle in front of foreigners but is gradually returning to be a part of normal Kazakh life.

PEOPLE OF KAZAKHSTAN

Without any doubt or exaggeration, the most interesting experience in Kazakhstan is meeting its people! Of course the historical sites and natural resources are important for any traveller, but the people and their attitude always sink into the soul much stronger. Whilst to some, the people of Kazakhstan may seem to be too serious or concerned only about their own affairs, it would be wrong to call them indifferent to the fate of the traveller. Often their concern (some would say - guardianship) may even seem overly excessive, and you may want a little bit more privacy. There is a belief that the hospitality of people is inversely proportional to the density of the population, and it is believed that in the case of Kazakhstan, with its immense and sparsely populated expanses, this is the ultimate truth. The farther away you move from the big cities, the more soulful and touching is local attitude towards the guest. An ordinary tourist becomes a wanderer; a wanderer has always been welcomed and treated properly in the East. At times, the generosity and selflessness of the Kazakh people is truly humbling.

KAZAKH YURT

You cannot claim to know the real Kazakhstan without having visited a real Kazakh yurt (kiz üy- "felt house"). This ancient nomadic dwelling, which is still used today in the life of Kazakhs, is one of the symbols of the country's heritage. Some cattle breeders move to the "zhailau" (summer pasture) in summer and from June to September live in yurts. You can see them in the mountainous regions usually, but also in the Mangyshlak region just east of the Caspian sea. Yurts are widely used as a mobile home during national holidays, including Nauruz and the national holidays in May. Sitting round a low table, draped in colourful cloth eating a traditional meal before sleeping on "tekemets" (felt carpets) under soft "corpe" (thick quilts) is an unforgettable activity to do in Kazakhstan.

The yurt has a spherical shape, which gives it a maximum heat efficiency. It is warm in winter and cool in summer. The wooden frame of the yurt, after it is installed and fixed, is covered with layers of felt that are attached to wooden poles with long cords. The most important part of the yurt is a round "shanyrak" at the top, which serves as the ventilation of the yurt and the exhaust for smoke from the burning stove located in the middle of the yurt. In addition to its practical purpose, the "shanyrak" plays an important symbolic role. It is inherited each generation; the word itself is used with the dual meaning of "hearth" and "home". It symbolises the unity of man with the cosmos. Lying at night under the open "shanyrak" and looking at the stars from the warmth of the yurt is a favourite pastime of many a visitor.

KAZAKH CEMETERY

A visit to any of the Kazakh cemeteries usually requires picking up a camera and staying at the facility for a long time. For steppe nomads of all ages, the only essential type of architecture was the architecture associated with the funeral for the deceased. Mazars (mausoleums) were erected in order to perpetuate the memory of ancestors and great people. The Mazar has always been more than a grave for the Kazakhs, functioning as a place of worship and somewhere to "talk" with the dead. Since ancient times, people have sought to bury relatives at the family cemetery, next to their ancestors. The erected shrines are very diverse in architectural design and material. Depending on the region, the building material varies but can be from almost anything—raw or baked brick, granite or limestone, logs or fences, and exotic bundles of reed stems. All of these are then covered with clay. Mazars may be round or square in shape, single or connected via corridors, with or without a dome; their design is limited only by imagination and economic conditions. The sizes of structures very clearly speak of the social situation of the deceased and his family.

KOKPAR

Kokpar, also known as "goat tearing," is a very old game, and no one knows for certain where it originated. Amongst the cultures of different Central Asian nations, it is called different names: Buzkashi, Kok-boru and Ulak-Tartysh. In Kokpar, the aim is to pick up the carcass of a headless goat from the ground while riding at full speed and then propelling it towards the goal. Previously, the goal would be a marked by a yurt but today tractor or truck tyres mark the "kazandyk", that is, the "cauldron". To win a point you have to throw the animal's carcass into this cauldron.

Kokpar can be either an individual (every man for himself) sport or involve a team. The first type involves mass participation and some games have seen as many as a thousand people involved. Understandably it is a very dangerous sport and many often come away with bad injuries in spite of all kinds of "armour" that the participants wear to try and protect themselves. Sadly it is not uncommon to hear of deaths as a result of the sport, but until you have seen the game played out in front of your eyes you will not be able to appreciate the lengths to which participants go to win the game and why they risk their lives in pursuit of their sport.

NAURUZ

In Kazakhstan, at the end of March, when the real heat has not yet started and the cold can return at any point, the Nauruz feast of spring and renewal is widely celebrated throughout the country. By experiencing this celebration you will certainly get your own piece of the spring mood, even if at the time of these events there may be unexpected snow.

The name of the holiday comes from the Persian "Nauruz," which means "new day." In Kazakhstan, the festival is celebrated for three consecutive days, from 21st to 23rd March with the main festivities usually falling on the 22nd. On this day, the main streets of big cities are blocked and scenes, yurts, and swings are installed. The presence of the number 7 is obligatory during the celebration of Nauruz in Kazakhstan. Therefore, on this day, according to Kazakh tradition, a special meal, "nauryz-koje", is cooked in every house, prepared from seven components (water, meat, salt, fat, flour, cereals, and milk).

OFF-ROAD EXPERIENCE WITH GAZ-66

Entertainment in the form of off-road riding in the back or on the roof of a GAZ-66 is not just for Kazakhstan, but is possible in all the former Soviet Union countries as a result of the legendary status of this machine. First produced in 1964, the military truck used by the Soviet army became extremely popular among the civilian population needing to reach remote places. Try to tell the locals that you are going to cross the nearby river in your sturdy jeep and they will warn you against it unless you are in a GAZ-66. The complete lack of comfort in a vehicle that at times appears not to have been designed for transporting people at all is compensated by its cross-country ability and the confidence that you will reach your destination no matter how demanding a journey it is. There are plenty of places to arrange a ride on a GAZ-66 in Kazakhstan, including Kapalskiy Izvoz in Jungar, Alatau, Bayankol Gorge, or the old Austrian road in Altai.

KAZAKH LANGUAGE

Salem
(Hello)

Sau-bol
(Goodbye)

Rakhmet
(Thank you)

The Kazakh language belongs to the Kypchak group of Turkic languages. The group includes the Tatar, Bashkir, Karachai-Balkarian, Kumykian, Karaimian, Crimean-Tatar, Karakalpakian and Nogay languages. The ones closest to Kazakh are Karakalpakian and Nogay. Nowadays the Kazakhs use Cyrillic characters from the Russian alphabet with 9 specific letters added. But it wasn't always that way: Arabic characters were in use until 1929 and the Roman alphabet - between 1929 and 1940. The debate about returning to Arabic characters or the Roman alphabet has been raging since Kazakhstan became an independent state. At the moment, taking into account the latest political statements, the Roman alphabet seems the most probable scenario.

Few Russians speak the Kazakh language and even the Kazakh people themselves don't always know it. The authorities try to introduce Kazakh language into public life, but it hasn't taken off yet. Right now you will definitely survive without Kazakh in Almaty or Astana, but visit a small village somewhere in South Kazakhstan and you will realise that just a few words are useful. Try to start with a couple of words and repeat them. "Salem" (hello), "sau-bol" (goodbye) or "rakhmet" (thank you) will open the hearts of local people even more.

Аа	Әә	Бб	(Вв)	Гг	Ғғ	Дд	Ее	(Ёё)	Жж	Зз
а	ә	бе	ве	ге	ға	де	йе	йо	же	зе
a	ä	b	v	g	ḡ	d	e	ë	ž	z
[a]	[æ]	[b]	[v]	[ɵ]	[g]	[d]	[iә]	[jo]	[ʒ]	[z]

Ии	Йй	Кк	Ққ	Лл	Мм	Нн	Ңң	Оо	Өө	Пп
ый/ій	қысқа и	ка	қа	эл	эм	эн	эң	о	ө	пе
i	j	k	ķ/kh	l	m	n	ņ	o	ö	p
[әj/әj]	[j]	[k]	[q]	[l]	[m]	[n]	[ŋ~ɴ]	[u̯ʊ]	[ẙɥ]	[p]

Рр	Сс	Тт	Уу	Ұұ	Үү	Фф	Хх	hh	(Цц)
эр	эс	те	ұу/үу	ұ	ү	эф	ха	hа	це
r	s	t	u	ū	ü	f	x	h	c
[ɾ]	[s]	[t]	[w/ʊw/ɥw/w/әw/әw]	[ʊ]	[ɥ]	[φ]	[χ;q]	[h]	[ts]

(Чч)	Шш	(Щщ)	(Ъъ)	Ыы	Іі	(Ьь)	(Ээ)	Юю	Яя
че	ша	ща	Ъ айыру	ы	і	Ь жіңішкелік	э	йу	йа
č	š	šč	белгі	у	ī	белгі	è	ju	ja
[tɕ]	[ʃ]	[ɕ]	''	[ә]	[ә]	'	[e]	[ju/jy]	[ja]

ASTANA PRO TEAM

Strong steppe winds across Kazakhstan's spacious countryside together with its mountainous terrain combine to produce Kazakh cyclists with international recognition because they always train in a head wind. So, there is no surprise, that Astana Pro Team, a professional road bicycle racing team, are one of the most positive and widely promoted brands of Kazakhstan. Founded in 2007, with the support of the then Prime-Minister of Kazakhstan Daniyal Akhmetov (who was also the president of the Cycling Federation of Kazakhstan at that time), the team has united the best Kazakh and foreign riders. The names of Alexander Vinokourov (aka Vino), Andrey Kashechkin and Maxim Iglinsky began to be famous both in Kazakhstan and abroad, and cycling as a sport acquired momentum in Kazakhstan. Celebrities such as Alberto Contador, Lance Armstrong, Levi Leipheimer and Vincenzo Nibali were invited to the team to make it even stronger. At the moment Alexander Vinokourov, the former rider of the team, is the general manager of Astana.

Cuisine

BESHBARMAK

Vegetarians can skip this page, because it would not be appealing. What is at issue is the main meal of Kazakh cuisine - Beshbarmak (Kazakhs themselves often just call it "yet"), which is made up primarily of horsemeat or mutton. A celebration party cannot be considered a holiday nor its guests important, if there is no "Beshbarmak".

The meat used in Beshbarmak is usually cooked for a long time on a low heat, making the broth ("sorpa") beautifully rich. Meat removed from the finished broth and cut into small pieces, and this time dough, rolled out into the thinnest flat cakes and cut into small squares, is boiled with onions in a broth. Then boiled dough laid out on a large dish, meat is laid in large quantities on top and broth poured upon with onions. At the last moment, eaters served hot broth.

Beshbarmak is usually served in an important ritual, according to the social role of the eaters – first the oldest or the most honoured guests, and then others. Translated it means "five fingers", because it is traditionally eaten with the hands with special parts reserved for the different guests. The boiled sheep's head is usually placed in front of the most honoured guest, while other parts have significance to other attendees with the children receiving the heart and kidneys, for example, which is believed to help them mature.

BAURSAKS

There is nothing particularly complicated needed to prepare baursaks, at least at first glance. The process of frying them is really quite simple, just drop into the pan for a few minutes before removing. The secret to a delicious baursaks, however, is how the dough is prepared. You'd be foolish to compete with a Kazakh chef whose hands might have made tens of thousands of baursaks, so just leave it to the experts.

What is a baursak? It is a small round or square donut with a hollow interior that is cooked by frying it in a cauldron or deep pan. Baursaks for most Kazakhs replaces bread and are served pretty constantly either as a separate snack with tea, where they can be eaten with salted butter or currant jam, or as a supplement to "sorpa" (soup).

KOUMISS

This fermented frothy milk drink of off-white colour and made from the milk of a mare is a rather peculiar experience to taste in Kazakhstan. Don't be put off by the fact that there are often small pieces of fat that can be seen floating in your cup. The sour-sweet and slightly bitter combination is something you will either love or hate!

Horse breeding nomads first engaged in the manufacture of koumiss from the fifth century B.C. and the drink is first mentioned in Herodotus' stories about the Scythians. Koumiss' alcoholic strength varies remarkably from 0.2% to 40%, but it has always been a drink for all occasions for Kazakhs who usually drink it at about 2.5% strength.
Koumiss' value lies in its medicinal properties: it is believed to improve metabolism, treat lung and intestinal diseases and cure illnesses of the nervous system. So important is its medical role that there are special koumiss-cure centres in Borovoye and Petropavlovsk.

TEA PARTY

Tea is undoubtedly one of the main and most universal expressions of Kazakh hospitality. A small bowl with tea is the first thing that is offered to the weary wanderer by every household. Kazakhs generally prefer black tea with, although in the south, closer to Uzbekistan, it is replaced by a green tea. Keep in mind that if someone offers you a cup of tea, you should not take the phrase too literally. Be prepared for the fact that one is not limited to serving just tea, with many visitors anticipating a warm brew being served vodka or koumiss instead! Tea is often supplied at the beginning of the meal. The traveller will be offered a wide choice of dishes to go with their tea such as candy, cookies, halvah, nuts, pastries, dried fruits, baursaks and oil, as well as a bunch of other dishes to keep the guest busy while the host prepares the main meal.

BLACK CAVIAR

The "Caviar Capital" of Kazakhstan is Atyrau (which is an oil capital as well). Both facts are confirmed on the modern emblem of the city, where sturgeons and an oil derrick are depicted. It is Atyrau where numerous photos of expats (working in local offices of Chevron, Agip, BP, etc.) with caviar were often taken about ten years ago. The majority of those photos had the same plot: a table with a big jar of black caviar on it and a happy smiling man, holding a huge tablespoon full of caviar. Times are changing though, and now caviar, even in Atyrau, is not so easy to obtain. They say that nowadays the average price of 1 kg of black caviar in Atyrau is a little bit more than 1000 US dollars, while in Almaty it is already 2000 US dollars. You should also know that commercial fishing for sturgeon is prohibited in the Caspian Sea as of 5 years ago. So, if you think of buying black caviar, be warned it is not a legal product. Poaching is a big industry in the Caspian region, do not support it, even if you want to make one of those notorious photos. There are plenty of other fish roe products that almost replace caviar, so you can still enjoy the tradition!

KAZY

For many people eating horse, a Kazakh nomad's best friend, may sound a bit too cannibalistic. But it is common for people in Kazakhstan, and is surprisingly tasty and very healthy. Kazy, a horse sausage, is mainly a festive meal, so you will definitely see its dark slices at weddings, birthdays and other celebrations. How to cook it? Simply take washed horse intestine and fill it with horse flesh and fat, together with spices (salt, pepper, cumin, and sometimes garlic). The meat is inserted into the intestine together with the rib, so the sausage always has a half-round form. This is then left in a cold place for 2 days or so. Finally kazy is usually boiled (for about 2 hours on a slow fire). It can also be smoked (12-18 hours) or jerked (about a week). In places like the Green Bazaar in Almaty, kazy can be prepared for cooking right in front of you.

History

ABAI PLACES

Many believe eastern Kazakhstan to be the spiritual centre of the country. This opinion has arisen because it was here that the most famous Kazakh poet and philosopher, Abai Kunanbayev, lived. As the author of poems and philosophical works, a talented translator, composer, educator and social activist, Abai was the founder of modern Kazakh written literature.

There is also the Zhidebay tract at the spurs of the Shyngystau Ridge in the Abai district of East Kazakhstan. This is where the family residence of Kunanbayev is located, which was bequeathed to Abai in 1884. It is in Zhidebai that he wrote most of his poems and translations. The same house is now a museum dedicated to Abai with interesting historical expositions. In the last century, the Zhidebai memorial complex, "Abai-Shakarim," was built, underneath which lay the remains of Abai and his relatives, some of whom, in particular, the poet and philosopher Shakarim Kudaiberdiev, also contributed to the Kazakh culture.

AISHA-BIBI MAUSOLEUM

Written sources do not contain any information about the history of the mausoleum of Aisha-Bibi, situated not far from Taraz. Only a legend exists about the romantic love of a brave soldier, Karakhan, and the beauty of Aisha and her nurse called Babaji Khatun. The most popular version of the legend ends with Aisha's death from a snake's bite, leading to Karakhan, in his grief, erecting a mausoleum in memory of his beloved and the dedication of her nurse, who promised to take care of the grave until her death.

The fame of the Aisha-Bibi mausoleum has brought its decoration: the entire surface of the building is a solid terra-cotta coating depicted with rich and diverse patterns. Babaji Khatun Mausoleum, located next to the first mausoleum, by contrast, is characterized by its simplicity of architectural composition. The local population has special affection for both mausoleums. The romantic aura surrounding them is obvious and the reason that it has become a custom for newly married couples to come here during the wedding ceremony and walk counter-clockwise past the mausoleums. People say that this act, preformed while praying, will save the couple from poverty and other ailments.

ANCIENT CITY OF SARAISHYK

The ancient city of Saraishyk (or Saraichik), located 50 kilometres north of modern Atyrau on the left bank of the Ural River, hosts the ruins of a large medieval city that once stood on a caravan route between the East and the West. Written records date the founding of Saraishyk to the 12th century, with the city gaining prosperity as the capital city of Batu Khan of the Golden Horde in the 13th century. Arab traveller and geographer, Ibn Battuta, was was greatly impressed during his visit, noting particularly the ferry transport system on the river. After destruction by Tamerlane in 1395, the city was revived as the capital of the Nogai Khanate, then the first Kazakh khans. Saraishyk is of particular importance for the history of the Kazakh people because here, according to legend, seven khans are buried. These Golden Horde Khans are Sartak, Berke, Toktakiya, Janibek (according to other sources Mangu Timur), Kazakh - Kasim, Nogai khans, and Izmail Uraz

ABAT-BAITAK MAUSOLEUM

According to legend, a mausoleum, which stands 12 kilometres south of the Taldysai settlement in the Aktobe region, was built during the Golden Horde era on the place where Batyr Abat died. He was the son of the legendary Kazakh utopian philosopher and poet, Asan Kaigy (Asan Sad). Legends recount his wars against the Kalmyks, during which he became famous. His life was cut short, however, during his wedding ceremony when the camel he was sitting on stumbled and he fell to his death. We are told that horrified onlookers and followers erected this magnificent monument in just three days.

The Abat-Baitak mausoleum was built in 14th-15th centuries out of mud brick and lined with baked square bricks. The original was about 16 metres tall and apparently sparkled with gold. Remnants of the original blue glaze can occasionally be seen amongst the cracks of the brickwork, but unfortunately time has faded its glory. Of particular interest is the necropolis, formed around the mausoleum over the centuries. The variety of tombstones are unique, containing floral and geometric patterns, the stamps of Kazakh tribes, pictures of weapons and jewellery and a great variety of decorative motifs to lose the visitor in its detail.

BEGAZY TOMBS

The mysterious granite tombs of Begazy have become the most famous archaeological discovery in the Central Kazakhstan. From this necropolis, located on the right bank of the river Karatal and south-west of the Kyzylarai mountains, began the study of Bronze Age culture.

The discovery of Begazy is credited to a luminary of Kazakh Archaeology, Alkei Margulan, who carried out his first excavation in 1947. At that time he discovered square tombs, built of slabs of about four feet in length, each weighing about three tons. It is believed that the tombs were erected during the highest period of Bronze Age culture, when society organised by tribal alliances. Their development was the result of a high level of metallurgy having been achieved. . If you go, try and see the tombs at sunset when the setting sun tinges the granite slabs with a mesmerising orange colour.

BOTAI SETTLEMENT

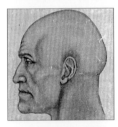

There has been much debate on where the horse was first domesticated. Kazakhstan, Russia and Saudi Arabia have all claimed in this role, among others. The settlement of ancient breeders, the Botai, was discovered 25 years ago in Northern Kazakhstan and is believed to be where man first settled into life in the saddle. The Botai settlement, located on the right bank of the Iman Burluk river belongs to the Eneolithic era. It is believed that people lived here in the third millennium B.C. Years of excavations have uncovered nearly 300,000 artefacts, including many related to the domestication of the horse For anyone interested in discovering more, we recommend you watch a very interesting documentary called, "The first horseman", which explores the Botai as its main theme. The story is led by pioneering archaeologist, Victor Seibert, who discovered the ancient settlement and dedicated his life to researching it.

GOLDEN MAN OF ISSYK

The Golden Man is one of the most popular symbols of Kazakhstan and one of the starting points for the new identity of Kazakhs. The name of the Issyk burial mound, where it was found, has become known around the world as the site of one of the greatest archaeological finds of the Saka (Scythian) period dating back to the 5th and 6th centuries B.C. Located on the outskirts of the town of Issyk, 50 kilometres east of Almaty, the burial mound was excavated in 1969. Here archaeologists discovered a grave lined with fir logs on the floor on which laid the remains of a Scythian warrior's ceremonial clothing, completely covered with 4,000 gold ornamental components. The headdress is tall and pointed, decorated with images of winged horses, snow leopards, mountain goats and birds. This warrior is likely to have been a prince, although his identity remains unknown.

Today, the site of discovery houses an open-air museum of "Saki mounds". The excavation of ancient burial grounds is not yet complete, which allows visitors the opportunity to watch them take place or even take part in them. Today the original Golden Man is kept in a state depository and copies are exhibited in virtually all the country's major historical museums.

GREAT GAME OF SHOKAN VALIKHANOV

Shokan Valikhanov went down in history as a great explorer of Central Asia, discovering a virtually unknown world surrounding the city of Kashgar. He carried out many expeditions to the region, studying data on the history, geography, and ethnography of the many peoples who inhabited this land in the middle of the 19th century. Valikhanov became one of the first Kazakhs to receive a European education and took the opportunity to combine modern knowledge with ancient traditions. During his short life (he died before he reached 30), Valikhanov managed to master many professions: traveller, writer, ethnographer, historian, geographer, military servant, artist, cartographer, and even intelligence officer – becoming a key participant of the famous Great Game rivalry between the British and Russian empires for dominance in Central Asia. In Kazakhstan, many places are associated with the name of Valikhanov. These are Semey, Almaty, the foothills of the Altyn-Emel and the mountain passes of the Tien Shan.

OLD URALSK

Uralsk, perhaps, is the city where the history of the foundation of Russian statehood on the Kazakh steppes has been most compactly preserved. In this western city of Kazakhstan, almost everything, including the most interesting buildings in the old part of the city, is connected with the Cossacks and Cossack troops of east Slavic origin.

The Golden Church (Cathedral of Christ the Saviour), has been the unofficial symbol of the city since it was founded with the assistance of the then Crown Prince and later the Russian Emperor, Nicholas-II, in 1891. It was built to celebrate the 300th anniversary of the creation of the Ural Cossack army. The southern edge of Uralsk, which is actually its historic centre, is called the "Kureni"; here almost every house is a monument because much of the area is built in the traditional Cossack wooden log style. Kureni is famous for two things: the Museum of Pugachev and an old church - Michael the Archangel Cathedral. The church was built in 1751 and its walls witnessed and survived the Peasant War led by Pugachev in the early 1770s. The museum of Pugachev is largely a museum of the Cossack way of life during those times.

THE MAUSOLEUM OF KHODJA AKHMED YASSAVI

The land of Southern Kazakhstan is rich in holy places, revered by Muslims and regarded as places of pilgrimage. However, the Mausoleum of Khodja Akhmed Yassavi, a famous poet, philosopher and preacher of Islam who became leader of the Sufi Order "Yassaviya", takes an honourable first place among them. Yassavi was one of those people who brought a "soft" and tolerant version of Islam to the steppe, which still prevails in Central Asia. This form of Islam did not promote or lead to the religious wars and witch-hunting seen in other offshoots.

The Mausoleum of Akhmed Yassavi, built in Turkestan at the turn of 13th-14th centuries, by order of Tamerlane himself, includes a number of areas, the most important of which are the gurkhana (tomb) of Ahmed, the "Jamaatkhana" meeting hall, a mosque, a mixture of large and small "aksaray" meeting areas, a "kitabkhana" (library), and "askhana" (dining room). The Jamaatkhana is considered the central hall and connects to the rest of the premises. At the centre is a huge ceremonial cauldron, a symbol of unity and hospitality. The Jamaatkhana is covered with the largest dome in Central Asia, which is 18.2 metres in diameter and the complex is deservedly a UNESCO World Heritage Site.

MANGYSTAU
UNDERGROUND "MOSQUES"

The legendary underground "mosques" in the Caspian region Magystau are the caves of preachers from the Sufi branch of Islam, rooted in these parts during the 14th century. They were cut into the limestone rocks in order to house Sufi teachers, their families, and students. Today, they are places of pilgrimage.

The Shakpak-Ata "Mosque", located on the Tub-Karagan peninsula, northeast of Fort-Shevchenko, is considered the most interesting place in cave architecture in Western Kazakhstan. The cave has been carved into the shape of a Latin cross consisting of four chambers, supported by four columns with capitals. On the portal and the inner walls of the underground mosque there are many inscriptions, images of animals and glyphs. Among the inscriptions a Sufi poem stands out, referring to the impermanence of the world and shortness of human life.

Interesting examples of similar architecture can also be seen at the Shopan-Ata mosque, which is surrounded by the largest ancient necropolis in Kazakhstan and located in the settlement of Seneca, more than 200 kilometres from the city of Aktau. This mosque was built by one of the disciples of St. Khodja Akhmed Yassavi, who also built the Becket Ata mosque and the mosque in the chalk rocks at Oglandy in the Western part of the Ustyurt Plateau.

90

PETROGLYPHS TAMGALY

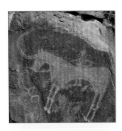

Bronze and Iron age rock carvings and images were found in the Tamgaly ravine, located in the south-eastern part of the Chu-Ili Mountains, in the late 1950s. Despite the fact that many petroglyphs have been found in different parts of Kazakhstan since, these have become the true classics. The name Tamgaly in Kazakh and various other Turkic languages means the "painted or marked place." The most famous images discovered show divine or shamanic figures with circular halos "of sun" around their heads. These images have become popular symbols in modern Kazakhstan.

The Tamgaly area covers approximately 10 kilometres and has nearly 5,000 paintings across the whole site filled with a number of side canyons to explore. Many different eras in the history of the human development are present including the Middle and Late Bronze ages (14th-12th centuries B.C.) and the Saks, Usun, and Turkic periods. Until recently, next to the main canyon, a military training ground was located. Sadly the ignorant manoeuvres of the armed forces over the years have led to significant destruction of many of the stone slabs containing petroglyphs. Today the site is included in the UNESCO list of World Cultural Heritage Sites and is protected, although previous restoration attempts have lost some of the authenticity of this former site of worship.

RUINS OF AKYRTAS

The ruins of Akyrtas are located in the south of the country, near Taraz, are one of the most interesting and mysterious structures ever discovered in Kazakhstan. The method of its construction does not resemble any of the many other settlements found on the territory of modern Kazakhstan: A rectangle with 138 and 162 metre sides. Inside the building the bases of 28 giant columns are found, each of which has a base measuring 5 metres by 5 metres. The sandstone blocks that were used in the construction of the exterior are 3 metres long. Despite many years of excavation and research, scientists have not been able to reach a consensus regarding the origin of this grand building. Meanwhile ordinary people cannot stop talking about the strong energy of this place and its salubrious properties. Some think that Akyrtas was built in the 8th century by the Arab commander, Qutayba, to provide a defensive fortress. Some believe that the Karluk Turkic tribe were responsible for its construction. There is also a hypothesis that a Buddhist monastery or Nestorian church may have been built there. One thing is clear, the foundation and the first rows of masonry that can be seen show the beginnings of a grand building, which, appears to have never been completed.

RUINS OF OTRAR

Between the cities of Turkestan and Shymkent, off a side road, is the village of Shaulder. Here there is one of the most interesting museums of Kazakhstan, dedicated to the history of Otrar, a great city on the Silk Road that in ancient times was as well known as Alexandria or Baghdad. Northeast from Shaulder, towards the pilgrimage site, Arystan Bab, are the ruins of this legendary city. The ancient settlement, near the confluence of the River Arys and Syrdarya, is being systematically excavated, so you will be able to touch the ancient stories. The stones around are beginning to "speak" of their history and you will hear the sounds of life in a large medieval city, as well as the sounds of the city being razed, to the ground in 1219.

Every Kazakh pupil is taught about the story of the heroic defence of Otrar, under the Mongol army siege that lasted more than six months, and was only taken as a result of betrayal by one of the military leaders. Everyone knows about the heroism of the governor Kair Khan and his men, who defended the Otrar to their last drop of blood. When the last stronghold fell, Kair Khan, forced back onto a roof, defended it to the last, using stones as weapons when the arrows ran out. Despite his bravery, he was captured alive and taken to Genghis Khan, who brutally ordered that molten silver be poured into Kair Khan's ears and eyes.

THE RUINS OF THE SAURAN FORTRESS

If you are moving from Turkestan to the north-west, towards Kyzylorda, about forty kilometres to the left of the road you can see the quite monumental ruins of an ancient fortress. It is a sight you cannot miss, for there are no more impressive looking ruins of a medieval city in the whole of Kazakhstan. It is believed that this city was founded by the Arabs around the 8th century A.D. on a site located three kilometres from the main settlement, which has been best preserved and is the more popular attraction these days. Later, for some reason, the old town was abandoned and the construction of a new one began, probably at the turn of the 12th-13th centuries. Surprisingly, despite having strong fortifications, Sauran did not resist the forces of Genghis Khan, preferring to surrender under a peace agreement with the Mongols and live under their protection. Later, in the 14th century, Sauran became the capital of the Juchi Ulus - Akorda, one of the states that emerged from the ruins of the Mongol Empire. This was an era of genuine prosperity in the region.

TEREKTY-AULIYE ROCK CARVINGS

The petroglyphs of Terekty-Auliye relate to the Bronze Age (second millennium B.C.), and are found dotted on flat granite outcrops located 80 kilometres northeast of Zhezkazgan. The most prevalent motifs are associated with animals, mostly horses, camels and oxen. The drawings are a reflection of the nomadic life of ancient people with stories devoted to hunting, wild animals and images that show them worshiping the sun. The technique used in drawing the image is of special interest to scientists studying early man. First the contour of the image was drawn and then the picture around the contour is smoothed with pebbles. There are many legends associated with Terekty Auliye which bring all manner of pilgrims to visit. To the west of the granite paintings there is an open-air museum for those interested in Kazakh Mazars, the resting places of noblemen and cultural figures from the 9th century.

TOMB OF GENGHIS KHAN'S SON

Juchi Khan (although under Kazakh tradition usually called Zhoshy) was the eldest son of Genghis Khan and the ancestor of most of the Kazakh khans. He especially loved the steppes of Sary-Arka and it was near the Ulytau mountains that he founded his main headquarters. The Khan's headquarters has long been a major administrative and cultural centre of the steppes. Not far from the spot where the ruins of the headquarters are found, there is also the mausoleum of Juchi, a square red brick building crowned with a blue dome and a portal with a lancet arch. It is believed that the mausoleum was built in the 14th or 15th century by one of the descendants of Juchi, although there are some who believe in an earlier period of construction; the date stamped on the tomb is 1227 (the year of the death of Ghengis Khan). According to popular legend, the eldest son of Genghis Khan was killed northeast of Ulytau while hunting. He was torn to pieces by a lame koulan (wild ass) that dragged the Khan from his horse and bit off his right hand. Historians, however, have other versions on the death of Khan and its perpetrators.

Soviet Heritage

LENIN IN KARAGANDA

10-15 years ago, this statue of the leader of the world proletariat, Ulyanov Lenin, could be seen in every city in Kazakhstan. Throughout the Soviet period, all the cities were full of these kinds of monuments, showing Lenin sitting and standing behind a rostrum, calling for something and pointing the way to a brighter future. However, in the years following the independence of Kazakhstan, such monuments have started to disappear, either removed entirely or transferred to less popular places.

Among the many monuments some were impressive such as the one in Karaganda, which, standing at a height of 12 metres and weighing about 800 tons, was considered the largest in Kazakhstan. Interestingly, it has also become the record holder for oldest existing monument of Lenin and was only dismantled by the authorities in 2011. Now the monument is located to the rear facade of the Lenin Cinema on Lenin Avenue in Karaganda. Judging by the amount of times the name of Lenin is used in the area, it is as though the whole place is still Lenin's!

RECORDS OF EKIBASTUS

The "Bogatir" coal mine, located near the town of Ekibastus, became the largest open-cut mine in the world when it was entered into the Guinness Book of Records in the 1980s having only been opened in 1970. The mine produces 56.8 million tons of coal, despite the fact that the rated capacity of the section was planned only to produce 50 million tons per year. The mine has provided for significant development of the local industry and settlements. In 1987 one of the tallest buildings in the industrial world was built here. The funnel of one of the coal-fired power plants, GRES-2, rising to a height of 420 meters, was also entered in the Guinness Book of Records. Whilst this may not be your usual tourist attraction, it is quite an important part of Kazkahstan's economic development history!

KARLAG

Karlag, whose full name is the Karaganda Corrective Labour Camp of the People's Commissariat of Internal Affairs, NKVD, was one of the hundreds of camps, which were collectively called the Gulag and were organized by Joseph Stalin during the period of mass political repression. There were other camps on Kazakhstan's territory, but Karlag stood out for its size and significance. The political prisoners that once inhabited the camps were used to create a workforce for the thriving coal and metallurgy industries. These days, it is quite simple to see the ruins of the former totalitarian machine. 40 kilometres south-west of the city of Karaganda lies Dolinka village, where, from 1931 to 1959, the administration of the camp was located. In the grandiose building of the former Administration of Karlag, built in the spirit of Soviet neo-classicism, a Museum dedicated to the victims of political repression is now located. There are many other interesting objects in the village that are associated with the camp - a former hospital for civilians and house officers, home appliances, a maternity ward, children's cemetery, a prayer hall and numerous adobe huts erected by the prisoners themselves.

SEMIPALATINSK TEST SITE

There are places on earth, in which just staying there you can literally feel their history on your skin. The "Opytnoye Pole" ("experimental field"), which is the part of the former Semipalatinsk nuclear test site, is one such place. The first Soviet nuclear explosion occurred at the Opytnoye Pole, 50 kilometres south-west of the town of Kurchatov, on August 29th 1949. It was the first test of a nuclear weapon, carried out by the Soviet Union, and balanced the power of the USA, creating a system of mutual nuclear deterrence between the USSR and the USA. Opytnoye Pole can be considered one of the most dangerous places in the scientific "Polygon" because the background radiation is hundreds of times higher than normal. However this does not make it inaccessible to the public and an experienced guide (which is mandatory) will show you some simple precautions to take so as not to impact your health and remain safe.

SHIPS IN THE DESERT

The Aral Sea is one of the notorious attractions in Kazakhstan for all the wrong reasons. Once one of the largest inland bodies of water in the world, the Aral Sea has all but evaporated. Today the walk from the former coastline villages to the present-day shore can be as much as 100-150 kilometres, such is the extent of the reduction in size. Initially the huge lake began to divide into two parts - the Large Aral Sea, which continues to decrease strongly, and the Small Aral. The cause of this separation was purely manmade as a result of the incredible expansion of irrigated agriculture in the Kara Kym and Kyzyl Kym desert. The flow of water from the region's two largest rivers, the Amudarya and Syrdarya, into the Aral Sea has virtually stopped. Today the vast territory occupied originally by the sea is a depressing area of saline waste. The drying of the sea has had a disastrous effect on the local economy, particularly the city of Aralsk, which once had a highly developed fishing industry. Today a "graveyard of ships" can be seen near the city. Amongst the rusty remains that once floated on the purest waters, camels now wander as the desert sands encroach. Gradually the rusty boats are being removed, some recycled and others dismantled for environmental reasons. A visit is nonetheless a chilling reminder of the speed of impact that man can have on nature if left unchecked.

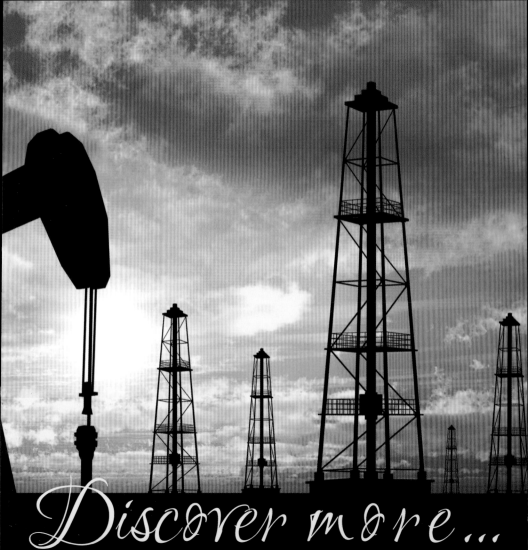

Discover more...

INDEX

You would be forgiven for missing the tiny landlocked country of Kyrgyzstan on the map. Meshed into Central Asia's inter-locking web of former Soviet Union boundaries, this mountainous country still has more horses than cars. It never fails to surprise and delight all who visit. Proud of its nomadic traditions, dating back to the days of the Silk Road, be prepared for Kyrgyzstan's overwhelming welcome of hospitality, received, perhaps, in a shepherd's yurt out on the summer pastures. Drink bowls of freshly fermented mare's milk with newfound friends and let the country's traditions take you into their heart. Marvel at the country's icy glaciers, crystal clear lakes and dramatic gorges set beneath the pearly white Tien Shan mountains that shimmer, heaven-like, in the summer haze as the last of the winter snows caps their dominating peaks. Immerse yourself in Central Asia's jewel with its unique experiences and you will leave with a renewed zest for life and an unforgettable sense of just how man and nature can interact in harmony..

Available on www.amazon.co.uk & www.discovery-bookshop.com

ISBN:978-0-9574807-4-2

Travelling around the world may appear as easy as A,B,C in the twenty first century, but looks can be deceptive: there is no 'X' for a start. Not since Xidakistan was struck from the map. But post 9/11, with the War on Terror going global, the sovereignty of 'The Valley' is back on the agenda. Could the Xidakis, like their Uzbek and Tajik neighbours, be about to taste the freedom of independence? Will Xidakistan once again take its rightful place in the League of Nations?

The Valley's fate is inextricably linked with that of Graham Ruff, founder of Ruff Guides. In a tale setting sail where Around the World in Eighty Days and Lost Horizon weighed anchor, our not-quite-a-hero suffers all the slings and arrows outrageous fortune can muster, in pursuit of his golden triangle: The Game, The Guidebook, The Girl.

With the future of Guidebooks under threat, The Alphabet Game takes you back to the very beginning, back to their earliest incarnations and the gamesmanship that brought them into being. As Evelyn Waugh's Scoop did for Foreign Correspondents the world over, so this novel lifts the lid on Travel Writers for good.

Wilson tells The Game's story with his usual mix of irreverent wit and historical insight, and in doing so delivers a telling satire on an American war effort.

THE ALPHABET GAME
by Paul Wilson

Paperback
RRP: £14.95
ISBN: 978-0-9927873-2-5

Available: www.amazon.co.uk
www.discovery-bookshop.com
also availbe on Kindle

The Guidebook is Dead?
Long Live the Guidebook.

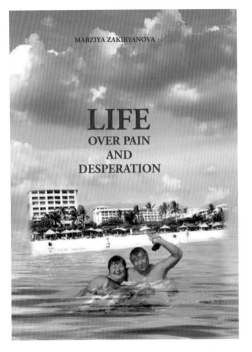

This book was written by someone on the fringe of death. Her life had been split in two: before and after the first day of August 1991 when she, a mother of two small children and full of hopes and plans for the future, became disabled in a single twist of fate.

Narrating her tale of self-conquest, the author speaks about how she managed to hold her family together, win the respect and recognition of people around her and above all, protect the fragile concept of 'love' from fortune's cruel turns.

By the time the book was submitted to print, Marziya Zakiryanova had passed away. She died after making the last correction to her script.

We bid farewell to this remarkable and powerfully creative woman.

Once alive, learn to survive

LIFE OVER PAIN AND DESPERATION
by Marziya Zakiryanova

Hardback
RRP: £14.50
ISBN: 978-0992787332

Available: www.amazon.co.uk
www.discovery-bookshop.com
also availbe on Kindle

An in-depth study of Genghis Khan from a Kazakh perspective, The Turkic Saga of Genghis Khan presupposes that the great Mongol leader and his tribal setting had more in common with the ancestors of the Kazakhs than with the people who today identify as Mongols. This idea is growing in currency in both western and eastern scholarship and is challenging both old Western assumptions and the long-obsolete Soviet perspective. This is an academic work that draws on many Central Asian and Russian sources and often has a Eurasianist bias – while also paying attention to new accounts by Western authors such as Jack Weatherford and John Man. It bears the mark of an independent, unorthodox and passionate scholar.

The book begins with a summary of the impact of the Eurasian nomads on world history and a sketch of how the dynamics of the steppe cultures interacted and came to rule, in many cases, the sedentary cultures that they conquered, creating characteristic two-tiered societies (Zakiryanov's 'KZ factor'). It then quickly goes on to examine the genealogy of Genghis Khan, the ethnicity of the various tribes close to him and the language they would have spoken. Drawing also on historical currents in China and Russia, and illustrated by the author's own present-day travels in Mongolia and throughout the Turkic world, Zakiryanov examines the origins and relationships of both the Kazakhs and the Mongols with each other and their neighbours.

THE TURKIC SAGA OF GENGIZ KHAN
by Kairat Zakiryanov

Hardback
RRP: £17.50 ·
ISBN: 978-0992787370

Available: www.amazon.co.uk
www.discovery-bookshop.com
also availbe on Kindle

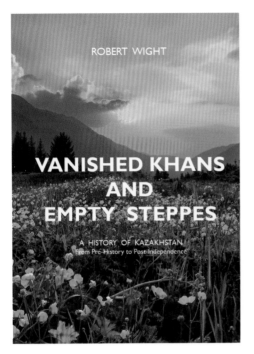

VANISHED KHANS AND EMPTY STEPPES
by Robert Wight

Hardback

This is a major new history of an increasingly important country in Central Asia.

The book opens with a brief history of the city of Almaty, from its nineteenth-century origins as a remote outpost of the Russian empire up to its present status as the commercial capital of present-day Kazakhstan. The story then goes back to the Neolithic and early Bronze Ages, and the sensational discovery of the famous Golden Man of the Scythian empire, before the siege and destruction of the ancient city of Otrar under the Mongol leader Genghis Khan. The emergence of the first identifiable Kazakh state in the sixteenth century is followed by early contacts with Russia, the country which came to be the dominating influence in Kazakhstan and Central Asia for over three hundred years. The book shows how Kazakhstan has been inextricably caught up, for better or worse, in the vast historical processes - of revolution, civil war, collectivisation, and the fall of communism - which have extended out from Russia over the past century. In the process it has changed dramatically, from a simple nomadic society of khans and clans, to a modern and cosmopolitan country. The transition has been painful and difficult for millions of people, but *Vanished Khans and Empty Steppes* illustrates how Kazakhstan has emerged as one of the world's few successful post-communist countries.

The Gods of the Middle World, the new novel by Galina Dolgaya, tells the story of Sima, a student of archaeology for whom the old lore and ways of the Central Asian steppe peoples are as vivid as the present. When she joints a group of archaeologists in southern Kazakhstan, asking all the time whether it is really possible to 'commune with the spirits', she soon discovers the answer first hand, setting in motion events in the spirit worlds that have been frozen for centuries. Meanwhile three millennia earlier, on the same spot, a young woman and her companion struggle to survive and amend wrongs that have caused the neighbouring tribe to avenge for them. The two narratives mirror one another, while Sima finds her destiny intertwined with the struggle between the forces of good and evil. Drawing richly on the historical and mythical backgrounds of the southern Kazakh steppe, the novel ultimately addresses the responsibilities of each generation for those that follow and the central importance of love and forgiveness.

Based in Tashkent and with a lifetime of first-hand knowledge of the region in which the story is set, Galina Dolgaya has published a number of novels and poems in Russian. The Gods of the Middle World won first prize at the 2012 Open Central Asia Literature Festival and is her first work to be available in English, published by Hertfordshire Press.

THE GODS OF THE MIDDLE WORLD
by Galina Dolgaya

Paperback
RRP: £14.95
ISBN: 978-0957480797

Available: www.amazon.co.uk
www.discovery-bookshop.com
also availbe on Kindle

Kazakhstan, the 9th largest country in the world, is a natural wonder that boasts endless steppes and deserts, high mountains (some more than 7000 meters) and large lakes. Here it is possible to see herds of wild Saigaks, Persian gazelles, Asian Wild donkeys, camels and horses. The country, once the home of free nomadic peoples was literally the crossroads of Asia, containing four different routs along the Great Silk Road. The nomadic influence is still very strong, despite years of Soviet urbanization. In rural areas many Kazakhs still live in their Yurtas -the traditional felt tents of the monadic shepherds.

"ASIA DISCOVERY LTD" is one of the leading tour operators in Kazakhstan with working experience of 15 years. Our company staff is professionally trained and skilled experts who are always trying to provide and ensure travel services at the highest level. "ASIA DISCOVERY LTD" conducts tours round the Almaty region, Kazakhstan. Within the city there are fast-flowing mountain rivers from snow-melt from the high glaciers, cutting their way through steep-sided valleys. Nearby there are waterfalls and beautiful Alpine meadows awash with multi-colored carpets of spring and summer flowers and grasses. In the Almaty region can also be found two of the largest National Natural Parks of Kazakhstan. An eye-pleasing landscape, a rich variety of flora and fauna, and friendly people who are proud of their tradition of hospitality and crafts will be with you throughout your tour.

"ASIA DISCOVERY LTD" Specializes in: Business tourism, Adventure tours; ethnographical, cultural, ecological, scientific (ornithological, botanical and entomological) tours and expeditions; horseback riding tours; trekking; mountain biking; water tourism(Rafting and boating); sport fishing; helicopter excursions and off-road tours, City and Week end tours.

"ASIA DISCOVERY LTD" provides the complete range of tourist services:
* Visa support;
* Organization of group and individual tours;
* Business tourism;
* Reservation and ticketing for domestic and international flights;
* Reservation of railway tickets;
* Hotel booking in Kazakhstan and Central Asia;
* MICE (Conferences, Seminars, Exhibitions);
* Events tourism (festivals, concerts, costume parties etc.);
* Corporate services;
* VIP services;
* Meeting-seeing off at airports, transfers to / from Hotels;
* Transport services in Kazakhstan and abroad;
* Organization of excursions, expeditions;
* Professional Guide and interpreter services;
* Scientific consultants for special tours.

Asia Discovery LTD
Office 19, 61 Abai Ave.
Almaty 050022 Kazakhstan
Tel: +7(327) 260-13-93, 2508-108.
Tel./Fax +7(327) 292-69-31
E-mail: info@asia-discovery.kz
Website: www.asia-discovery.kz

КАЗАҚТЫҢ СПОРТ ЖӘНЕ
ТУРИЗМ АКАДЕМИЯСЫ

КАЗАХСКАЯ АКАДЕМИЯ
СПОРТА И ТУРИЗМА

"University Sports:
Nation's health and
prosperity"

International Association of Universites
of Physical Culture and Sport
83/85 Abay Avenue, Almaty
Republic of Kazakhstan, 050022
tel/fax: +7 727 239 06 51
e'mail: iasuni@inbox.ru
web site: www.iasuni.com

The warmth of native hearth away from home!

The hotel "OTRAR" **** is located in the very center of Almaty, opposite the wonderful Park area, shopping - and business centers, "Akbota" Amusement Park and City Zoo, 20 minutes to International airport, 5 minutes walk to subway station "Zhibek Zholy" and also 5 minutes to nearest railway terminal-2.

ACCOMMODATION

The hotel has 161 comfortable rooms ready to accommodate up to 200 people. All rooms are equipped with air-conditioners, en-suite bathrooms, International telephone comminication, satellite TV, refrigerators, mini-bars, hair dryers and deposit safes.
WiFi, Gym – free for our guests.

Visa support & Registration Services, Airport pick-up and drop service,
Excursions, VIP service at the Airport

ADDRESS

Republic of Kazakhstan, 050002, Almaty 73, ul. Gogolya.
Tel.: +7 (727) 2506806, 2506848, 2506830, 2506840
Fax: +7 (727) 2506809, 2506811
e-mail: otrar@group.kz ; otrarhotel@mail.ru
www.group.kz

LUXURY
LIFESTYLE
MAGAZINE

Editorial

Almaty, Kazakhstan

 +7 727 354 34 10

 +7 701 228 64 10

 info@dorogoe.kz

WWW.DOROGOE.KZ

Hotel
ALPINIST
Kyrgyzstan   Bishkek

113 Ranfilov Street, Bishkek, Kyrgyzstan
Tel.: +996-312-699 621   Fax: +996-312-595 647
E-mail:alpinist@elcat.kg   www.alpinist.centralasia.kg

ASIA HOTELS

Many Cities - One Chain

ASIA TASHKENT

Tashkent, Usmon Nosir str., 111, 70059
Tel./Fax: + 99871 2509680
E-mail: tashkent@asiahotels.uz
www.asiahotels.uz

ASIA SAMARKAND

Samarkand, Kosh Hauz str., 50, 140100
Tel./Fax: + 998 662 358230
E-mail: samarkand@asiahotels.uz
www.asiahotels.uz

Marco Polo
Central Asia travel
Owner of Asia Hotels Chain
www.marcopolo.uz

ASIA BUKHARA

Bukhara, Mekhtar Ambar str., 20018
Tel./Fax: + 99865 2246431
E-mail: bukhara@asiahotels.uz
www.asiahotels.uz

ASIA FERGHANA

Ferghana, Navoi str., 26A, 150100
Tel./Fax: + 998 732 245221
E-mail: ferghana@asiahotels.uz
www.asiahotels.uz

ASIA KHIVA

Khiva, Yakubova str., 220900
Tel./Fax: + 998 623 757683
E-mail: khiva@asiahotels.uz
www.asiahotels.uz

Silk Road ADVENTURES

All travel across the Central Asia.

Tourist Company
"Silk Road Adventures"
050012, Kazakhstan, Almaty
Adi Sharipova Str., 117- 44
Tel./fax: + 727 268 27 43
Mobile phone: + 7 702 340 33 19
infosra@silkadv.com
moldirsra@silkadv.com
alexandrsra@silkadv.com
www.silkadv.com

AITMATOV ACADEMY

Kazakh Arts

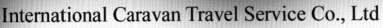

open central asia

society
culture
travel
business

Building landbrige with Central Asia

www.ocamagazine.com

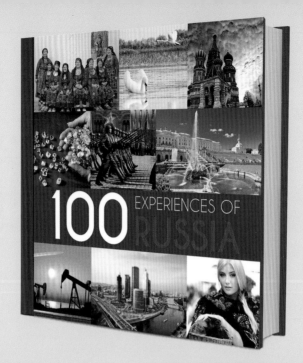

COLLECT EXPERIENCES NOT THINGS!

COMING SOON ...